WO

CAMPAIGN
English for the military

Yvonne Baker de Altamirano
Simon Mellor-Clark

MACMILLAN

Macmillan Education
Between Towns Road, Oxford OX4 3PP
A division of Macmillan Publishers Limited
Companies and representatives throughout the world

ISBN 978-1-4050-0982-9

Designed by Keith Shaw, Threefold Design
Layout by Carolyn Gibson
Cover design by Keith Shaw, Threefold Design
Cover photograph by Alamy Images

The authors would like to thank all colleagues at the Academia
General Militar, Zaragoza; not only teachers and military instructors
in the Department of English, but also military personnel from other
departments who have helped with suggestions and explanations.
Thanks also to Jorge, Daniel and Rubén Altamirano for all their
patience and support.

The publishers would like to thank Louis Harrison and Shona Rodger
for all their hard work.

The authors and publishers would like to thank the following for
permission to reproduce their photographs:
Corbis p 18; Hulton Archive p 37; Military Picture Library
International pp 3, 4, 14, 19, 24, 29, 34, 36, 39, 42, 47, 52, 57, 62, 67, 72,
77, 80; MOD photo library p20.

Cover image by Doug Steley / Alamy Images

Picture research by Kevin Brown

Printed in Thailand

2015   2014   2013
12 11 10 9 8 7

Contents

① Start point

glossary Military vehicles

Task 1 Translate.

armoured personnel carrier /ˈɑːməd pɜːsəˈnel ˌkæriə(r)/ (APC) (n) /eɪpiːˈsiː/
helicopter (n) /ˈhelɪˌkɒptə(r)/
infantry fighting vehicle /ˈɪnfəntri ˈfaɪtɪŋ ˌviːəkl/ (IFV) (n) /aɪefˈviː/
jeep (n) /dʒiːp/
plane (n) /pleɪn/
tank (n) /tæŋk/
truck (n) /trʌk/

Task 2 Put the words into groups.

vehicles: 1 *armoured personnel carrier*   2 ....   3 ....

4 ....   5 ....

aircraft: 6 ....   7 ....

Jobs

Task 3 Translate.

airman (n) /ˈeəmən/
doctor (n) /ˈdɒktə(r)/
engineer (n) /ˌendʒɪˈnɪə(r)/
interpreter (n) /ɪnˈtɜːprɪtə(r)/
journalist (n) /ˈdʒɜːnəlɪst/
police officer (n) /pəˈliːs ˌɒfɪsə(r)/
sailor (n) /ˈseɪlə(r)/
soldier (n) /ˈsəʊldʒə(r)/
teacher (n) /ˈtiːtʃə(r)/

Task 4 Circle six jobs.

Q	K	M	B	D	C	W	O
S	A	I	L	O	R	E	F
O	I	P	Z	C	J	K	F
L	R	A	B	T	D	F	I
D	M	U	V	O	W	F	C
I	A	N	M	R	I	S	E
E	N	G	I	N	E	E	R
R	P	Q	S	R	Y	X	W

alpha

Task 1 Write *'m* (*am*), *'s* (*is*) or *'re* (*are*).

Hello. My name is Elaine.

Pleased to meet you. I am Max Bell.

Hello. You are my partner.

Good morning. We are from CNN.

This is Tom. He is American.

Hello. My name (1) *'s* Elaine.

Pleased to meet you. I (2) .... Max Bell.

Hello. You (3) .... my partner.

Good morning. We (4) .... from CNN.

This is Tom. He (5) .... American.

Task 2 Write *'m* (*am*), *'s* (*is*) or *'re* (*are*).

1 Hello. I'*m* Captain Reynolds.

2 Pleased to meet you. My name .... Fraser.

3 This is Kush. He............... my friend.

4 We .... from Britain, but they .... from Pakistan.

5 I .... from the USA.

Task 3 Complete.

Hanif: Hello, (1) .... Hanif.

Elaine: Pleased to (2) .... you. My (3) ....'s Elaine.

Hanif: Pleased to meet you.

bravo

Task 1 Write the nationalities.

	Country	Nationality
1	Poland	*Polish*
2	Britain	....
3	The USA	....
4	France	....
5	Pakistan	....
6	Algeria	....

Task 2 Write *'m not, aren't* or *isn't*.

1 Rayna's Polish. She *isn't* Russian.

2 Hanif's Pakistani. He .... Indian.

3 I'm British. I .... American.

4 We're Algerian. We .... Moroccan.

5 Ebru and Banu are Turkish. They .... Hungarian.

charlie

Task 1 Complete the jobs.

1 Fatima's a   d o c t o r.

2 Stefan's an   _ n g _ n _ _ r.

3 Harry's an   _ _ r m _ n.

4 Liz is a   j _ _ r n _ l _ st.

5 Abdul's a   s _ l d _ _ r.

Task 2 Answer.

1 Is Fatima a doctor? *Yes, she is.*

2 Is Stefan a sailor? ....

3 Is Harry a police officer? ....

4 Is Liz a journalist? ....

5 Is Abdul a soldier? ....

Task 3 Complete. Use *a* or *an*.

1 Liz is *a* British journalist.

2 Harry's .... American airman.

3 Stefan's .... French engineer.

4 Abdul's .... Pakistani soldier.

5 Fatima's .... Algerian doctor.

delta

Task 1 Put the words in the correct order.

1 you? | How | are   *How are you?*

2 thanks, | and | Fine | you? .... ?

3 well, | I'm | very | thanks ....

4 family? | is | your | How .... ?

5 you | well, | They're | very | thank ....

Task 2 Complete. Use these words.

> next week   weekend   ~~day~~   tomorrow

1 Well, have a nice *day*!

2 Goodnight! See you .... !

3 Harry: Bye, Jane. Have a nice ....

   Jane: See you .... !

echo

Task 1 Complete. Use *he's*, *she's*, *his* or *her*.

1   *His* name's Stefan. *He's* French. *He's* an engineer.

2   .... name's Liz. .... from Manchester. .... a British journalist.

3   .... name's Fatima. .... an Algerian doctor. .... friend's a doctor, too.

4   .... name's Abdul. .... a soldier. .... from Pakistan.

Task 2 Write the questions.

Pandit Patel

Doctor

7 Lotus Avenue, Karachi, Pakistan
telephone: 927 9764
e-mail: ppatel@medics.com

---

1   *What's his name*? It's Pandit Patel.

2   .... ? He's a doctor.

3   .... ? He's from Pakistan.

4   .... ? It's 7 Lotus Avenue, Karachi.

5   .... ? It's 927 9764.

6   .... ? It's ppatel@medics.com.

foxtrot

Task 1 Write the numbers.

0   *zero*

1 *one*	6	11	16 ....
2	7	12	17 ....
3	8	13	18 ....
4	9	14	19 ....
5	10	15	20 ....

Task 2 Write the numbers.

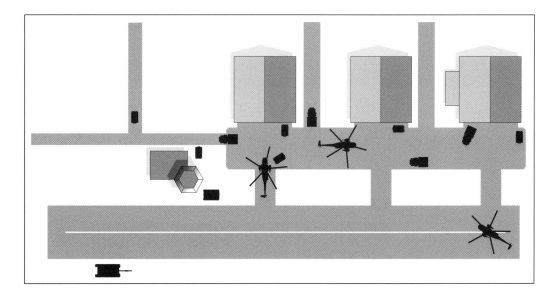

1   There is *one* tank.

2   There are .... jeeps.

3   There are .... trucks.

4   There is .... IFV.

5   There are .... helicopters.

listening

Task 1 [1] 💿 **Listen and write the letters.**

1 ....   2 ....   3 ....

4 ....   5 ....

Task 2 [2] 💿 **Listen and number.**

☐ the USA   ☐ an IFV

☐ the UN   ☐ CNN

☐ an APC

Task 3 Put the conversation in the correct order.

A | 1 | Excuse me, are you Mary Smith?

A | ☐ | No, I'm not. I'm from Canada.

A | ☐ | Oh, I'm sorry. What's your name?

A | ☐ | Where are you from, Barbara?

B | ☐ | Barbara. Barbara Stevens.

B | 2 | No, I'm not. That's Mary over there.

B | ☐ | Me? I'm from London. Are you American?

[3] 💿 **Now listen and check.**

Task 4 [4] 💿 **Listen and repeat.**

0 1 2 3 4 5 6 7 8 9 10 11 12 13 14 15 16 17 18 19 20

Task 5 [5] 💿 **Listen and write the numbers.**

1 ....   2 ....   3 ....   4 ....   5 ....   6 ....

Task 6 [6] 💿 **Listen and circle the correct information.**

Good (1) *morning / evening*. My name is Ivan (2) *Dancing / Danzig*. That's Ivan –
I-V-A-N Danzig – D-A-N-Z-I-G. I'm a (3) *sailor / soldier* in the Polish (4) *navy / army*.
I'm (5) *18 / 19*.

Task 7 [7] 💿 **Listen and complete the form.**

Name:	(1) Liz _____
Address:	(2) The Grand _____ , _____
Telephone no:	(3) _____
Job	(4) _____

Boot camp

glossary Basic combat training

Task 1 Translate.

barracks (n) /ˈbærəks/
basic combat training (BCT) (n) /ˌbeɪsɪk ˈkɒmbæt ˌtreɪnɪŋ/
combat uniform (n) /ˈkɒmbæt ˌjuːnɪfɔːm/
communications training (n) /kəˌmjuːnɪˈkeɪʃənz ˌtreɪnɪŋ/
drill (n) /drɪl/
field training exercise (FTX) (n) /ˈfiːld ˌtreɪnɪŋ ˈeksəsaɪz/
first aid (n) /ˌfɜːst ˈeɪd/
foot march (n) /ˈfʊt ˌmɑːtʃ/
graduation (n) /ˌgrædʒuˈeɪʃən/
instructor (n) /inˈstrʌktə(r)/
map reading (n) /ˈmæp ˌriːdɪŋ/
military skills (n) /ˌmɪlətri ˈskɪlz/
NBC training (nuclear, biological and chemical) (n) /ˌenbiːˈsiː ˌtreɪnɪŋ/
obstacle course (n) /ˈɒbstəkl ˌkɔːs/
recruit (n) /rɪˈkruːt/
wake up (n) /ˈweɪkʌp/ = reveille (n) /rɪˈvæli/
weapons training (n) /ˈwepənz ˌtreɪnɪŋ/
volunteer (n) /vɒlənˈtɪə(r)/

Task 2 Write five words with *training*.

1 *basic combat training*   2 ....   3 ....

4 ....   5 ....

Personal items

Task 3 Translate.

battery (n) /ˈbaetrɪ/
deodorant (n) /diˈəʊdərənt/
electric razor (n) /ɪˌlektrɪk ˈreɪzə(r)/
padlock (n) /ˈpædlɒk/
shampoo (n) /ʃæmˈpuː/
shaving cream (n) /ˈʃeɪvɪŋ kriːm/
shoe polish (n) /ˈʃuː pɒlɪʃ/
soap (n) /səʊp/
sun cream (n) /ˈsʌn kriːm/
toothbrush (n) /ˈtuːθbrʌʃ/
toothpaste (n) /ˈtuːθpeɪst/
towel (n) /ˈtaʊəl/

Task 4 Tick the items you have in your toilet bag.

alpha

Task 1 Complete.

> sleep ~~wear~~ teach go train

1 Soldiers *wear* a uniform.
2 They .... with weapons.
3 They .... in barracks.
4 We .... home at the weekend.
5 NCOs .... military skills.

Task 2 Make negative.

1 Policemen *don't live* in barracks. (live)
2 They .... military uniforms. (wear)
3 They .... drill. (do)
4 They .... to war. (go)

Task 3 Complete.

A alpha
B bravo
C charlie
D (1) ....
E echo
F foxtrot
G golf
H (2) ....
I india
J juliet
K kilo
L (3) ....
M mike
N november
O oscar
P (4) ....
Q quebec
R romeo
S sierra
T (5) ....
U uniform
V victor
W whiskey
X x-ray
Y yankee
Z (6) ....

Task 4 Write.

1 X98 *x-ray nine eight*
2 R50 ....
3 CPL ....
4 A2D ....
5 O90 ....

bravo

Task 1 Answer the questions.

1 Do army recruits wear a uniform? *Yes, they do.*
2 Do they go home during basic training? *No, they don't.*
3 Do they train with weapons? ....
4 Do they live at home? ....
5 Do they sleep in barracks? ....

Task 2 Match.

1 Do you live
2 Do they do
3 Do we go
4 What days do we
5 Are you a

a home tomorrow?
b civilian?
c have weapons training?
d in barracks?
e drill on Mondays?

charlie

Task 1 Write the plurals.

1 battery *batteries*

2 toothbrush ....

3 map ....

4 compass ....

5 padlock ....

6 country ....

Task 2 Match the numbers.

forty-five	sixty-three	ninety-eight	seventy-two	twenty-four	fifty-nine

63   95   45   24   72   98   42   59   54   36   27   89

thirty-six	eighty-nine	twenty-seven	forty-two	ninety-five	fifty-four

delta

Task 1 Write C for countable or U for uncountable.

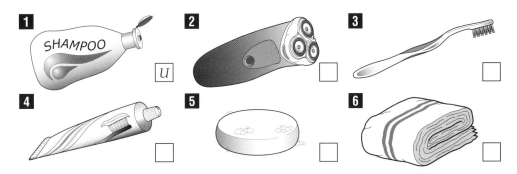

Now complete the sentence.

There is (1) *some shampoo,* (2) *an electric razor,* (3) .... ,

(4) .... , (5) .... and (6) ....

Task 2 Complete. Use *a* or *any*.

1 Does he have *a* razor?

2 There isn't *any* sun cream.

3 Does he have .... toothbrush?

4 Is there .... soap?

5 He doesn't have .... toothpaste.

6 Is there .... towel?

7 There aren't .... batteries.

8 There isn't .... padlock.

Task 3 Write the questions.

1 *How much are the maps?* They're $2.65.

2 *How much is the towel?* It's $13.

3 .... ? It's $15.

4 .... ? They're $3.

5 .... ? They're $5.

6 .... ? It's $1.50.

Special Offers! ▶ ▶ ▶ ▶

radio	$15	batteries	$3
towel	$13	maps	$2.65
padlocks	$5	deodorant	$1.50

echo

Task 1 Complete the questions. Use *What, Where* or *When*.

1   *What* time do you have breakfast?

2   .... do the recruits go at 11 am?

3   .... do we have dinner – at 9 pm?

4   .... do the soldiers do at 6 am?

5   .... time do you have lunch?

Timetable	
Reveille	6.00 am
Breakfast	6.30 am
Barrack Inspection	7.00 am
Training	7.15 am
Lunch	12.20 pm

Task 2 Write the questions. Then write the answers.

1   he / get up?

What time does he get up? He gets up at six o'clock.

2   he / have breakfast?

....

3   he / start training?

....

4   he / eat lunch?

....

foxtrot

Task 1 Complete the sentences.

London	12.00 pm
Paris	1.00 pm
Lima	6.00 am
Sydney	9.00 pm
Tokyo	8.00 pm
New York	7.00 am

At twelve hundred hours in London …

1   It's *thirteen hundred hours* in Paris.

2   It's .... in Lima.

3   It's .... in Sydney.

4   It's .... in Tokyo.

5   It's .... in New York.

Task 2 Complete. Use *on* or *at*.

1   Does the library close *at* 1700 *on* Mondays?

2   The museum doesn't open .... Tuesday mornings.

3   The club serves breakfast .... 0715 hours.

4   The club doesn't close until 2300 hours .... Saturdays.

5   The PX closes .... 2000 hours from Monday to Friday.

6   Lunch is .... 1300 hours .... Fridays.

Timetable	
Lunch	1220
Training	1330
Dinner	1700
Training	1830
Personal time	2030
Lights Out	2200

Task 3 Answer the questions.

1   Does he have lunch at twelve twenty? *Yes, he does.*

2   Does he have personal time before dinner? ....

3   Does he train before dinner? ....

4   Does he have uniform inspection in the afternoon? ....

5   Does he go to bed before 11 pm? ....

listening

Task 1 [8] 🔊 Listen and write the call signs.

1 ....   4 ....

2 ....   5 ....

3 ....

Task 2 [9] 🔊 Listen and number.

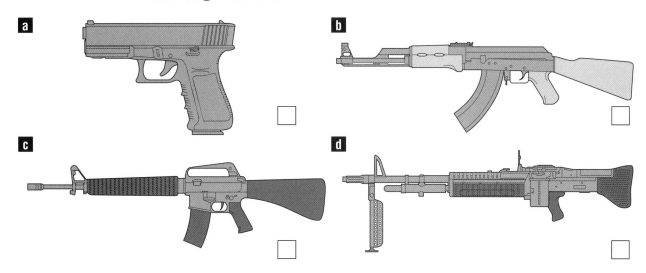

a □

b □

c □

d □

Task 3 [10] 🔊 Listen and complete.

TRAINING SCHEDULE	
Lunch	1200 – (1) ....
First aid	(2) .... – 1430
Foot march	1440 – (3) ....
Dinner	(4) .... – (5) ....
Communications training	1820 – (6) ....
Personal time	(7) .... – (8) ....
Lights out	2200

Task 4 [11] 🔊 What does Private O'Brien need? Listen and tick.

1 soap □ 2 toothpaste □ 3 toothbrush □

4 shampoo □ 5 towel □ 6 batteries □

Task 5 [12] 🔊 Listen and correct. There are four mistakes.

Reveille	0700
Personal hygiene	0600 – 0615
Breakfast	0615 – 0650
Barrack and uniform inspection	0700 – 0720
Training	0720 – 1220
Lunch	1220 – 1420

3 To be a soldier

glossary — Military career verbs

Task 1 Translate.

to be assigned (to) (vb) /əˈsaɪnd/ *They were assigned to a new unit.*
attend (vb) /əˈtend/ *I attended a First Aid class.*
to be deployed (to) (vb) /dɪˈplɔɪd/ *His regiment was deployed to Bosnia.*
enter (vb) /ˈentə(r)/ *She entered the Academy in 1997.*
graduate (from) (vb) /ˈgrædʒuˌeit/ *I graduated from Officer School in 1999.*
join (vb) /dʒɔɪn/ *He joined the navy when he was seventeen.*
to be posted to (vb) /ˈpəʊstɪd/ *They were posted to Germany.*
to be promoted (to) (vb) /prəˈməʊtɪd/ *He was promoted to the rank of captain.*
serve (in) (vb) /sɜːv/ *We served in UNPROFOR for two years.*
to be transferred (to) (vb) /trænsˈfɜːrd/ *He was transferred to Travis Air Base.*

Task 2 Write five verbs with *to be*.

1 *to be assigned* 2 .... 3 ....

4 .... 5 ....

Military uniform

Task 3 Translate.

badge (n) /bædʒ/
belt (n) /belt/
beret (n) /ˈbereɪ/
boots (n) /buːts/
cap (n) /kæp/
cap badge (n) /ˈkæp bædʒ/
epaulette (n) /ˈepəlet/ *(on the shoulder of the jacket of a military uniform)*

helmet (n) /ˈhelmɪt/
jacket (n) /ˈdʒækɪt/
name tag (n) /ˈneɪm tæg/
shirt (n) /ʃɜːt/
shoes (n) /ʃuːz/
skirt (n) /skɜːt/
trousers (n) /ˈtraʊzəz/

Task 4 Write three things to wear on your head.

1 .... 2 .... 3 ....

alpha

Task 1 Write sentences.

1 Charles Lindbergh (1902–1974) American pilot

Charles Lindbergh was an American pilot. He was born in 1902 and he died in 1974.

2 Che Guevara (1928–1967) Argentinian revolutionary

....

....

3 Erich Hartmann (1922–1995) German pilot

....

....

Task 2 Complete the sentences. Use *wasn't/weren't* or *was/were*.

1 Bernard Montgomery *wasn't* born in India. He *was* born in London, in 1887.

2 Nimitz and Lindbergh .... Russian. They .... from the USA.

3 Che Guevara .... born in Bolivia. He .... from Argentina.

bravo

Task 1 Read about Akbar the Great. Complete the dates for his life.

Akbar the Great (1) .... – (2) ....

Akbar the Great was an Indian Emperor. He was born in India in 1542. His full name was Jalal ud din Mohammed Akbar Ghazi.

In 1556, his father died in an accident. Akbar was now the Emperor. India was very big and it was a difficult country to lead, but Akbar was an intelligent leader. He was very tolerant, too. There weren't many wars during this time and he was very popular. When he died in 1605, he was 63 years old.

Now read the text again and answer the questions.

1 Where was Akbar the Great born? *He was born in India.*

2 What was his full name? ....

3 When was Akbar the Emperor of India? ....

4 How old was he when he died? ....

Task 2 Answer the questions.

1 Was Akbar the Great a Roman Emperor? *No, he wasn't.*

2 Was Akbar from India? ....

3 Was India a big country? ....

4 Was Akbar a bad leader? ....

5 Were there many wars in India during this time? ....

charlie

Task 1 Complete. Use the past simple.

1   He *joined* the army when he was twenty. (join)

2   He .... the NCO school at the age of twenty-two. (enter)

3   They .... overseas when he was in the army. (serve)

4   We both .... from West Point. (graduate)

5   They .... the officers' course. (attend)

Task 2 Complete. Use the past simple negative.

1   He *didn't join* the army when he was twenty. (join)

2   He .... the NCO school at the age of twenty-two. (enter)

3   They .... overseas when he was in the army. (serve)

4   We .... from West Point. (graduate)

5   They .... the officer school. (attend)

delta

Task 1 Write questions.

1   I enjoyed the party. What about you? *Did you enjoy the party?*

2   We had a good meal at the restaurant. What about you?

....

3   We went to Hakim's wedding. What about Hamsa?

....

4   Terry played for the Rockets. What about Martin and Steve?

....

5   I stayed at home yesterday. What about you?

....

Task 2 Put the words in order.

1   did I do I Sunday? I last I you I What   *What did you do last Sunday?*

2   did I celebrate I Hassim I birthday? I How I his

....

3   did I leave I last Saturday? I José and his friends I What time

....

4   did I do I What I yesterday? I your mother and father

....

5   did I go I last night? I Where I you

....

Task 3 Write *P* for the possessive form or *is* for the verb *be*.

1   Laura is Jack's ⎡*P*⎤ girlfriend. She's ⎡*is*⎤ from The Philippines.

2   Jack's ⎡ ⎤ a pilot in the US Air Force. It's ⎡ ⎤ an interesting career.

3   His brother's ⎡ ⎤ wife is an interpreter. She's ⎡ ⎤ Egyptian.

4   Jack's ⎡ ⎤ mother's ⎡ ⎤ a teacher, but his father's ⎡ ⎤ in the Air Force.

echo

Task 1 Make the sentences negative.

1 The recruits got up at 5 am. *The recruits didn't get up at 5 am.*

2 Joe wore a uniform. ....

3 They followed the orders. ....

4 The NCO saluted the colonel. ....

5 We did our exercises. ....

Task 2 Circle the correct form of the verb.

1 We *get* / *got* up very early yesterday.

2 They *wear* / *wore* their new uniform at the ceremony last Saturday.

3 I didn't *go* / *went* home last weekend.

4 We didn't *do* / *did* any exercises in the morning.

5 Their superior *give* / *gave* them some extra training yesterday.

foxtrot

Task 1 Tick the verbs.

	wash	clean	iron	polish	brush
boots		✔		✔	✔
belt					
jacket					
badge of rank					
trousers					
shirt					
beret					

Task 2 Complete. Use the past simple.

1 The soldiers *got up* at first light. (get up)

2 They .... their beds and .... a wash and shave. (make, have)

3 They .... on their uniform and .... outside. (put, go)

4 They .... their exercises and .... some water. (do, drink)

5 They .... the area. (leave)

Task 3 Answer the questions about Task 2.

1 Did the soldiers get up at first light? *Yes, they did.*

2 Did they make their beds? ....

3 Did they iron their uniforms? ....

4 Did they do their exercises in the PX? ....

5 Did they drink water? ....

listening

Task 1 [13] 🔘 **Put the verbs into groups. Then listen and check.**

started   trained   served   worked   marched   stopped   finished   celebrated   died

/t/	/d/	/ɪd/

Task 2 [14] 🔘 **Complete. Use these words. Then listen and check.**

party   club   birthday

A   Hi, there. Did you have a good weekend?

B   Yes, I did. It was my son's first (1) ....

A   Oh, really? How did you celebrate?

B   We had a big (2) .... for him.

A   What did you do last weekend?

B   I went to the (3) ....

A   Oh, really? I didn't see you!

Task 3 [15] 🔘 **Listen and tick the correct information.**

1   Yuri Gagarin was a Russian pilot. ☐

2   When he was 18 or 19, he joined a local flying club. ☐

3   His first assignment as a pilot was in Star City. ☐

4   He was in space for about 150 minutes. ☐

5   He had an accident in a new MiG-15. ☐

6   He died in his bed. ☐

Task 4 [16] 🔘 **Listen and complete the form.**

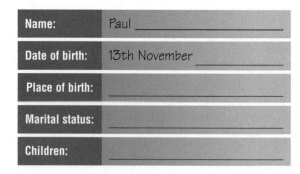

Name:	Paul _____
Date of birth:	13th November _____
Place of birth:	_____
Marital status:	_____
Children:	_____

Task 5 [17] 🔘 **Listen and circle.**

1   Where was Jack Truman born?   Niagara   Sacramento   Glendale

2   Where did he go for Boot Camp?   Niagara   Sacramento   Glendale

3   Where was his first duty station?   Niagara   Sacramento   Glendale

4   When was he deployed to Germany?   1992   1993   1995

5   How does he feel about his career in the Air Force?   Happy   OK   Unhappy

Military organisation

glossary Officer ranks

Task 1 Translate.

NATO	BRITISH ARMY	abbreviation	US ARMY	
OF-10	Field Marshal	FM / GOA	General of the Army	/ˈfiːldmɑːʃl/
OF-9	General	Gen	General	/ˈdʒenrəl/
OF-8	Lieutenant General	Lt Gen	Lieutenant General	/lefˌtenənt ˈdʒenrəl/ *UK* /luːˌtenənt ˈdʒenrəl/ *US*
OF-7	Major General	Maj Gen	Major General	/ˌmeɪdʒə(r) ˈdʒenrəl/
OF-6	Brigadier	Brig	Brigadier General	/ˌbrɪgəˈdɪə(r)/
OF-5	Colonel	Col	Colonel	/ˈkɜːnl/
OF-4	Lieutenant Colonel	Lt Col	Lieutenant Colonel	/lefˌtenənt ˈkɜːnl/ *UK* /luːˌtenənt ˈkɜːnl/ *US*
OF-3	Major	Maj	Major	/ˈmeɪdʒə(r)/
OF-2	Captain	Capt	Captain	/ˈkæptɪn/
OF-1	Lieutenant	(Lt) 1Lt	First Lieutenant	/lefˈtenənt/ *UK* /ˌfɜːrst luːˈtenənt/ *US*
OF-1	Second Lieutenant	(2/Lt) 2Lt	Second Lieutenant	/ˌsekənd lefˈtenənt/ *UK* /ˌsekənd luːˈtenənt/ *US*

Task 2 Answer the questions.

1 What is the British equivalent of the general of the US Army? *field marshal*

2 What is the American equivalent of a brigadier in the British Army? ....

3 What is the NATO grade of a major? ....

4 What is the abbreviation for a lieutenant colonel? ....

Army units

Task 3 Translate.

corps (n) /kɔː/ *A corps has between 40,000 and 60,000 men.*
division (n) /dɪˈvɪʒn/ *A division has between 10,000 and 20,000 men.*
brigade (n) /brɪˈgeɪd/ *A brigade has between 5,000 and 7,000 men.*
regiment (n) /ˈredʒɪmənt/ *A regiment has between 2000 and 6000 men.*
battalion (n) /bəˈtæljən/ *A battalion has between 500 and 1,000 men.*
company (n) /ˈkʌmpəni/ *An infantry company has between 100 and 200 men.*
platoon (n) /pləˈtuːn/ *An infantry platoon has between 30 and 40 soldiers.*
squad (n) /skwɒd/ *An American infantry squad has between 8 and 12 soldiers.*
section (n) /ˈsekʃən/ *A British infantry section has between 8 and 10 soldiers.*

Task 4 Put in order.

	■	■	■
1 platoon, section, company	*company*	*platoon*	*section*
2 division, corps, brigade	....	....	....
3 battalion, regiment, brigade	....	....	....

alpha

Task 1 Write the rank.

Lieutenant
Captain
Lieutenant Colonel
~~Major~~
Lance Corporal
Sergeant

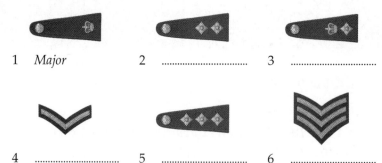

1   *Major*   2   3   ....

4   5   6   ....

Task 2 Complete the sentences.

1   A *lieutenant* commands a platoon. He's the *platoon commander.*

2   A .... is second-in-command (2IC) of a platoon.

3   A .... commands a company. He's 2IC of a battalion.

4   A .... is 2IC of a company.

5   A .... commands a battalion.

Task 3 Match.

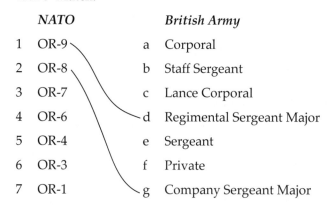

NATO	British Army
1 OR-9	a Corporal
2 OR-8	b Staff Sergeant
3 OR-7	c Lance Corporal
4 OR-6	d Regimental Sergeant Major
5 OR-4	e Sergeant
6 OR-3	f Private
7 OR-1	g Company Sergeant Major

bravo

Task 1 Add the abbreviation for the ordinal numbers.

1   2*nd* lieutenant

2   101........... Airborne

3   The 3........... rifle platoon

4   On 11........... November

5   The 8........... unit

6   The 14........... Signal Regiment

Task 2 Complete the puzzle and find the key word.

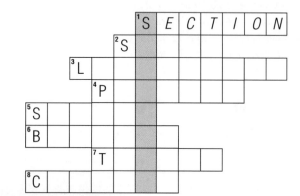

1   An infantry unit of 8 to 10 men.
2   The American equivalent of a section of the British army.
3   The officer in command of a platoon.
4   An infantry unit of 30 to 40 officers and men.
5   2IC = ... in command.
6   An artillery unit equivalent to an infantry company.
7   The name for armour, artillery and engineer units.
8   An infantry unit with three rifle platoons.

charlie

Task 1 Circle the correct word.

1 Sergeant to female captain:

   (Ma'am) / Miss, could I have a minute?

2 Sergeant major to private:

   A Private Hayes!

   B Yes, *sir / Lieutenant*.

3 Lieutenant colonel to general:

   Excuse me, *General / sir*, Captain Bryant is here to see you.

4 Lieutenant to corporal:

   A Corporal Sayek reporting for duty, sir.

   B Good morning, *Corporal / sir*. At ease.

5 NCO to private:

   Close the door, *Thomson / Private Thomson*.

delta

Task 1 Match.

1 When did you arrive in Helsinki?   a Yes, it is.

2 How long are you here for?   b It's nice and clean.

3 Is this your first visit to the city?   c We arrived last night.

4 What do you think of it?   d Just for the conference.

Task 2 Complete the dialogue. Use these words.

| is   what   do   ~~when~~   did   are |

Jean   (1) *When* did you arrive in Helsinki, Jan?

Jan   I arrived last night. (2) .... about you? When (3) .... you get here?

Jean   Oh, I arrived yesterday, too. How long (4) .... you here for?

Jan   Oh, just for three days. (5) .... this your first visit?

Jean   Yes, it is.

Jan   What (6) .... you think of the place?

Jean   I really like it.

Task 3 Complete the sentences. Use *for, in* or *at*.

1 She works *in* Geneva *in* Switzerland.

2 Dr Mornay works .... the World Health Organisation.

3 I work .... the NATO headquarters, ... Brussels.

4 I think they are .... the intelligence department.

echo

Task 1 Match.

1 The mission of the engineers is —————— a to operate the communication systems.

2 The mission of the intelligence corps is \ b to provide medical support.

3 The mission of the medical corps is c to build roads and bridges.

4 The mission of the signals unit is d to collect information about the enemy.

Task 2 Complete the text. Use these verbs.

> attack ~~operate~~ transport command provide fly collect

The mission of the Army Air Corps (AAC) is to (1) *operate* and to (2) ....

all the British Army's helicopters. The main function of the AAC helicopters is to

(3) .... enemy armour, but they are also useful for other missions, for

example, to (4) .... from the air, to reconnoitre and (5) ....

information, to (6) .... troops, supplies and equipment and to

(7) .... medical support.

foxtrot

Task 1 Answer the questions. Use these numbers.

> about 730   30–40   ~~8–10~~   8–12   about 16,000   236–313   100–200

1 How many soldiers are there in a section in the British army?
There are between 8 and 10 men in a section in the British army.

2 How many soldiers are there in a squad in the US army?

....

3 How many soldiers are there in a platoon?

....

4 How many soldiers are there in a company?

....

5 How many soldiers are there in a battalion?

....

6 How many officers are there in a brigade?

....

7 How many NCOs and soldiers are there in a division?

....

Task 2 Write.

1 Pl means *platoon*.   4 Bde means ....

2 Coy means ....   5 Div means ....

3 Bn means ....   6 Cav means ....

listening

Task 1 [18] 🎧 Listen and number.

a ☐   b ☐   c ☐   d ☐   e ☐

Task 2 [19] 🎧 Listen and write the number of the Army units.

> **Units deployed in the area**
>
> .... Armoured Brigade
>
> .... Cavalry Regiment
>
> .... Airborne Corps
>
> .... Infantry Division
>
> .... Signal Regiment
>
> .... Artillery Regiment

Task 3 [20] 🎧 Listen and complete the table.

NAME	ORGANISATION	DATE OF ARRIVAL	ETA
Mrs Hidas	MOD	(1)	(2)
Lt. Col. Moore	NATO	(3)	(4)
Gen. Akamoto	Japanese Defence Force	(5)	(6)

Task 4 [21] 🎧 Listen and complete. Use these words.

> Infantry   Signal   Medical   Engineers

Arms and services of the US Army

COMBAT ARMS

– Directly involved in fighting.
The Combat Arms include:
(1) _____ , Armor, Air Defense Artillery, Field Artillery, Aviation, Special Forces and Corps of (2) _____ .

COMBAT SUPPORT UNITS

– Provide operational assistance to the Combat Arms.
These units include:
(3) _____ Corps, Military Police Corps, Chemical Corps and Military Intelligence.

COMBAT SERVICE SUPPORT BRANCHES

– These include:
Transportation, Civil Affairs, Quartermaster, Finance, Army
(4) _____ Corps and Ordnance.

glossary

Sports

Task 1 Translate.

baseball (n) /ˈbeɪsbɔːl/
basketball (n) /ˈbaːskɪtˌbɔːl/
boxing (n) /ˈbɒksɪŋ/
climbing (n) /ˈklaɪmɪŋ/
football (n) /ˈfʊtbɔːl/
golf (n) /gɒlf/
karate (n) /kəˈrɑːti/
push-ups (n) /ˈpʊʃʌps/

running (n) /ˈrʌnɪŋ/
sit-ups (n) /ˈsɪtʌps/
skiing (n) /ˈskiːɪŋ/
swimming (n) /ˈswɪmɪŋ/
table-tennis (n) /ˈteɪbl ˌtenɪs/
tennis (n) /ˈtenɪs/
volleyball (n) /ˈvɒliˌbɔːl/
weight-lifting (n) /ˈweɪtˌlɪftɪŋ/

Task 2 Write seven ball games.

1 *baseball*   2 ....   3 ....   4 ....

5 ....   6 ....   7 ....

Assault course

Task 3 Translate.

cargo net (n) /ˈkɑːgəʊ ˌnet/ *Climb up the cargo net.*
ditch (n) /dɪtʃ/ *Jump across the ditch.*
fence (n) /fens/ *Climb over the fence.*
high wall (n) /ˌhaɪ ˈwɔːl/ *Climb up the wall.*
logs (n) /lɒgz/ *Run over the logs.*
low wall (n) /ˌləʊ ˈwɔːl/ *Jump over the low wall.*
ramp (n) /ræmp/ *Run down the ramp.*
rope (n) /rəʊp/ *Climb up the rope.*
tunnel (n) /ˈtʌnl/ *Run through the tunnel.*
wire (n) /waɪə(r)/ *Crawl under the wire.*

Task 4 Match.

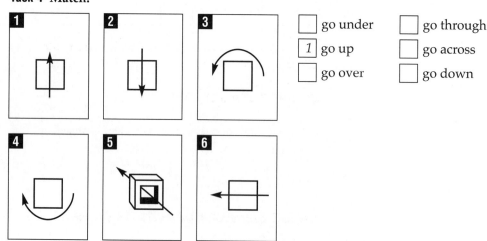

☐ go under   ☐ go through
1 go up   ☐ go across
☐ go over   ☐ go down

alpha   Task 1 Complete.

1 He's *lifting* weights in the gym. (lift)

2 She's .... sit-ups. (do)

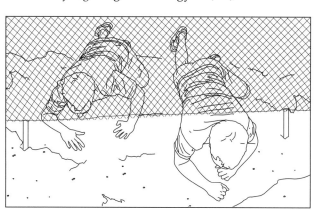

3 They're .... the assault course. (practise)

4 She's .... round the base. (run)

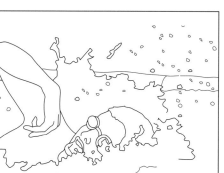

5 He's .... in the pool. (swim)

6 They're .... volleyball. (play)

bravo   Task 1 Look at the pictures and answer the questions.

1 Is the soldier in picture number 1 lifting weights?   *Yes, he is.*
2 Is the soldier in picture number 2 doing push-ups? *No, she isn't. She's doing sit-ups.*
3 Are the soldiers in picture number 3 crawling under the wire? ....
4 Is the soldier in picture number 4 running? ....
5 Is the soldier in picture number 5 swimming in the pool? ....
6 Are the soldiers in picture number 6 playing football? ....

charlie

Task 1 Complete. Use these words.

> bat caps racket shorts sports bag
> tracksuit trainers (×2) ~~T-shirt~~

The man is wearing a white (1) *T-shirt*, grey

(2) .... and white (3) ....

He's carrying a baseball (4) .... and a

(5) .... The woman is wearing a grey

(6) .... and black (7) ....

She's carrying a tennis (8) .... They are

both wearing baseball (9) ....

delta

Task 1 Complete the sentences. Use *likes, doesn't like* or *doesn't mind*.

	Yevgeny	Dieter
watching films	☺	☺
playing sports	☺	☹
reading magazines	😐	☹
watching football on TV	☹	😐
going out for a meal	☹	☹
listening to music	☺	☺
playing computer games	😐	☺

1 Yevgeny *likes* watching films and playing sports, he *doesn't mind* playing computer games, but he *doesn't like* watching football on TV.

2 Dieter doesn't like playing sports, but he .... playing computer games and he .... watching football on TV.

3 Yevgeny likes listening to music and he .... reading magazines, but he .... going out for a meal.

4 Dieter .... reading magazines or going out for a meal.

Task 2 Answer the questions.

1 Does Dieter like watching films? *Yes, he does.*

2 Does Yevgeny like playing sports? ....

3 Does Yevgeny like watching football on TV? ....

4 Does Dieter like going out for a meal? ....

echo

Task 1 Make sentences. Use the words in brackets.

1   I go swimming every week. (usually)
    I usually go swimming every week.

2   We play golf. (once a week)

    ....

3   I do weight-lifting. (every morning)

    ....

4   They go to the gym. (often)

    ....

5   He does sit-ups. (never)

    ....

Task 2 Complete. Use the present simple or continuous.

1   We usually *do* 50 push-ups, but today we*'re doing* 20. (do)
2   The soldiers .... table-tennis at the moment. (play)
3   The sailors .... up the ropes every morning before breakfast. (climb)
4   The men never .... round the base in the morning. (run)
5   Today we .... for the competition. (practise)

foxtrot

Task 1 Match. Then complete the sentences. Use these words.

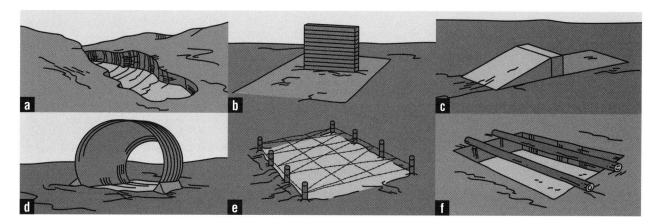

```
down   into   across   over   through   under   up
```

1   Run *across* the logs. [*f*]
2   Run .... the ramp and jump .... [ ]
3   Crawl .... the wire. [ ]
4   Jump .... the ditch and climb out. [ ]
5   Crawl .... the tunnel. [ ]
6   Jump .... the low wall. [ ]

listening

Task 1 [22] 💿 Listen and tick the correct picture.

Task 2 [23] 💿 Listen and tick the things he does.

ACTIVITY	✔	How often?
sit-ups		
weight-lifting		
basketball		
fencing		
volley ball		
golf		
swimming		
running		
table-tennis		

[23] 💿 Now listen again and write how often he does the activities.

Task 3 [24] 💿 Listen and number.

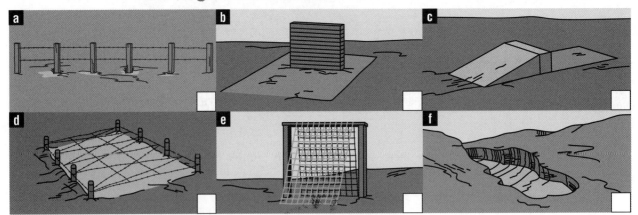

Task 4 [25] 💿 Listen and write true or false.

1 Some soldiers are crawling over the bridge. ....

2 Some soldiers are crawling through the long grass. ....

3 Two soldiers have some wire. ....

4 The two soldiers are carrying nets. ....

5 They're preparing an ambush. ....

A visitor to the base

glossary

Places

Task 1 Translate.

barracks (n) /ˈbærəks/ *Soldiers sleep in this building.*
base (n) /beɪs/ *An area with buildings for the military.*
cookhouse (n) /ˈkʊkhaʊs/ *The army cooks prepare the soldiers' food here.*
guardroom (n) /ˈɡɑːdrʊm/ *A room for soldiers on guard.*
headquarters (n) /ˈhedˌkwɔːtəz/ HQ /eɪtʃˈkjuː/ *The commanding officer and his assistants work here.*
main gate (n) /ˌmeɪn ˈɡeɪt/ *You enter the base from the street at this point.*
married quarters (n) /ˈmærɪd ˌkwɔːtəz/ *Accommodation for married soldiers and their families.*
Officers' Mess (n) /ˌɒfɪsəz ˈmes/ *Officers have their meals in this building.*
parade ground / square (n) /pəˈreɪd ˌɡraʊnd / skweə(r)/ *Troops assemble here for inspection and training.*
quarters for single soldiers (n) /ˌkwɔːtəz fə ˈsɪŋɡl ˌsəʊldʒə(r)z/ *Accommodation for single soldiers.*
training area (n) /ˈtreɪnɪŋ ˌeəriə/ *Soldiers practise field exercises here.*

Task 2 Answer the questions.

1 Where do you enter a military base? *At the main gate.*

2 Where do the officers have their meals? ....

3 Where do the soldiers practise drill? ....

People

Task 3 Translate.

adjutant (n) /ˈædʒʊtənt/ *This officer is responsible for administration in the HQ.*
Battalion 2IC (n) /bəˌtælɪən ˈsekənd ɪŋkəˌmɑːnd/ *This is the second officer in command of the battalion.*
commanding officer (n) /kəˌmɑːndɪŋ ˈɒfɪsə(r)/ *This officer commands, or is in charge of the unit.*
company commander (n) /ˌkʌmpəni kəˈmɑːndə(r)/ *This officer commands, or is in charge of, a company.*
cook (n) /kʊk/ *This person prepares the food.*
duty officer (n) /ˈdʒuːti ˌɒfɪsə(r)/ *This officer is responsible for security and communications during a 24-hour period.*
intelligence officer (n) /ɪnˈtelɪdʒəns ˌɒfɪsə(r)/ *This officer is responsible for information about the enemy.*
NCO (n) /ensiːˈəʊ/ *A non-commissioned officer (a corporal or sergeant).*
ops officer (n) /ˈɒps ˌɒfɪsə(r)/ *This officer manages operational planning in the Battalion HQ.*
platoon sergeant (n) /pləˈtuːn ˌsɑːdʒənt/ *This sergeant is 2IC of the platoon.*
quartermaster (n) /ˈkwɔːtəmɑːstə(r)/ *This officer is responsible for supplies at the barracks.*
security guard (n) /sɪˈkjʊərəti ˌɡɑːd/ *This soldier protects a building.*
signals officer (n) /ˈsɪɡnəlz ˌɒfɪsə(r)/ *This officer is responsible for the communications systems.*

Task 4 Name the people.

1 Who is in charge of administration at the battalion HQ? *The adjutant.*

2 Who is responsible for the communications systems? ....

3 Who commands a company? ....

alpha

Task 1 Write *guard* or *adjutant*.

1 He assists the commanding officer in the battalion HQ. *adjutant*

2 This soldier isn't usually an officer. *guard*

3 He doesn't always carry his weapon when he works. ....

4 He always carries his weapon when he's on duty. ....

5 He often works outside the buildings. ....

6 He's in charge of administration. ....

7 Sometimes he works near the main gate. ....

Task 2 Complete. Use these words.

weather   time   ~~flight~~   base   taxi

1 Did you have a nice *flight* from Athens?

2 Did you come by .... from the airport?

3 Is this your first .... in Brussels?

4 How was the .... in Athens?

5 What do you think of our .... ?

Now match the answers with the questions.

a [ ] Yes, it is.

b [1] Yes. It was twenty minutes late, but that was OK.

c [ ] It's great. I'm very impressed!

d [ ] Oh, it was nice.

e [ ] Yes, that's right. I got one immediately. No problem.

bravo

Task 1 Circle the correct word.

Right men, the barracks are here. We think about twenty men sleep in (1)(*this*)/ *that* building here. The cookhouse is over there and (2) *that / those* is the sergeants' mess right next to it. (3) *This / These* men are special forces. And (4) *these / those* troops on the parade ground over there are from the Regiment. This is the main entrance right (5) *here / there* and there's a guardroom there – (6) *this / that* is the security guard over there.

charlie

Task 1 Complete the sentences. Use *in, to, on, of* or *with*.

1 The Regiment is based *in* Shropshire.

2 Soldiers go .... operations overseas once or twice a year.

3 The unit is currently .... exercise in Germany, and is assigned .... a mechanized brigade.

4 It is equipped .... IFVs.

5 The HQ platoon consists .... a medical section and an intelligence section.

6 It is currently attached .... UN forces and stationed .... Europe.

Task 2 Complete the sentences. Use these words.

> commanded   provided   ~~led~~   inspected   organised   equipped

1 A squad is *led* by a corporal.

2 The troops are .... every morning on the parade ground.

3 Fire support is .... by the artillery.

4 The Recce platoon is .... with SCIMITAR reconnaissance vehicles.

5 A company in the British army is .... by a major.

6 The Army is .... into various units.

Task 3 Put the words in order.

1 not | tanks | The | unit | with | is | equipped
The unit is not equipped with tanks.

2 UN | assigned | The | are | to | troops | the

....

3 promoted | was | I | to | two | after | years | sergeant

....

4 regiment | stationed | The | is | Germany | in

....

Task 4 Read and answer the questions.

Airborne Infantry

9 Regiment Army Air Corps is stationed at Dishforth, in North Yorkshire, England. It has two anti-tank squadrons, and a light battlefield helicopter (LBH) squadron. There is also an aviation workshop, where the helicopters are repaired. At the moment, these squadrons provide combat power with Lynx mark 7 helicopters and use the TOW missile system. They also have Gazelle helicopters for reconnaissance missions.

---

1 Where is 9 Regiment Army Air Corps stationed? *At Dishforth, in North Yorkshire.*

2 How many squadrons does the Regiment consist of? ....

3 Which helicopters is the Regiment equipped with? ....

4 Which missile system is used? ....

5 Which missions are Gazelle helicopters deployed for? ....

delta

Task 1 Read and mark the places on the map.

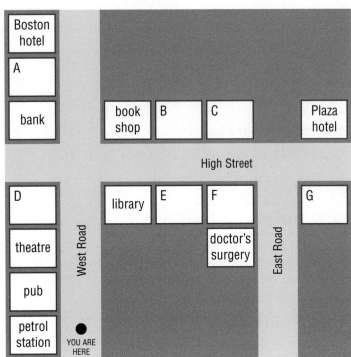

| Indian restaurant | Italian restaurant | leisure centre |
| cinema | police station | supermarket | pharmacy |

1 The supermarket is in the High Street next to the book shop.
2 The leisure centre is next to the library and opposite the supermarket.
3 There is a pharmacy in the High Street between the supermarket and the hotel.
4 The Italian restaurant is in the High Street, opposite the pharmacy, and the Indian restaurant is on West Road, between the bank and the hotel.
5 The police station is on the corner of the High Street and East Road.
6 The cinema is next to the theatre, on the corner of West Road.

Task 2 Read the directions and write true or false. (Start from the petrol station.)

1 Go along West Road and take the first right. The leisure centre is on the right, just after the library.
2 Go along West Road and take the second on the left. The supermarket is next to the Italian restaurant. You can't miss it.
3 Go straight on and when you get to the corner, turn right. Go along the High Street to East Road and turn right again. The petrol station is on the corner of the street, opposite the Plaza Hotel.
4 Walk up this road, cross the High Street and go straight on. I think the Indian restaurant is on the left, next to the Boston Hotel.
5 Walk up this street and turn right into the High Street. The hotel is opposite the police station. You can't miss it.

echo

Task 1 Complete the text. Use these words.

| airfields | amphibious | ~~bridges~~ | minefields | parachute |

The Royal Engineers help the Army and the other Services to live, move and fight. In combat, they build or destroy (1) *bridges*, and lay or clear (2) .... Behind the combat area, they build bridges, roads and (3) .... , and provide electricity. Engineering units are organised into Mechanized, Armoured, (4) .... , Air Support and (5) .... squadrons.

foxtrot

Task 1 Match.

1 An intelligence officer is responsible   a for a battalion.
2 A quartermaster manages   b of a company.
3 An adjutant assists   c combat support.
4 An officer commanding is in charge   d the logistics of the battalion.
5 A commanding officer is responsible   e for information about the enemy.
6 The headquarters company organises   f with administration in the battalion HQ.

listening

Task 1 [26] 🔊 Listen and match.

1	schedule	a	Sgt Brooks
2	transport to the airport	b	Sgt Harris
3	a driver	c	Cpl Smith
4	first aid equipment	d	Cpl Hayne
5	food	e	Sgt Briggs
6	maps, GPS and reconnaissance	f	the medic

Task 2 [27] 🔊 Listen and write true or false.

1 The situation is not difficult. ....
2 There's no gas or electricity. ....
3 The shops are open. ....
4 The banks are closed. ....
5 There isn't much food. ....
6 The airport is closed. ....

Task 3 [28] 🔊 Listen and mark the routes: A, B and C.

A = Thomas, Briggs and Hayne
B = Brooks, Harris and Smith
C = You (you are the new recruit)

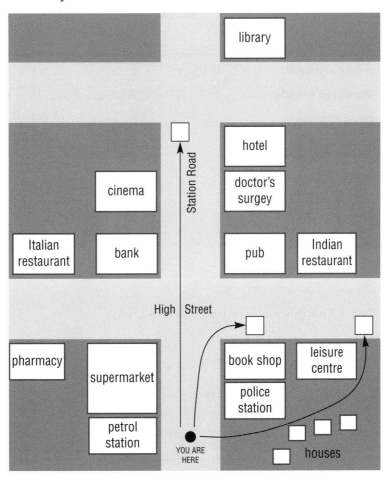

Task 4 [29] 🔊 Listen. Are the opinions positive (P) or negative (N)?

1 your office ☐   2 our office ☐   3 the flight ☐
4 the weather ☐   5 the city ☐   6 the people ☐

glossary — Aircraft, vehicles and naval ships

Task 1 Translate.

aircraft carrier (n) /ˈeəkrɑːft ˌkæriə(r)/
anti-tank weapon (n) /ˌæntiˈtæŋk ˌwepən/
APC (armoured personnel carrier) (n) /ˌeɪpiːˈsiː (ˈɑːməd pɜːsəˈnel ˌkæriə(r))/
bomber (n) /ˈbɒmə(r)/
destroyer (n) /dɪˈstrɔɪə(r)/
frigate (n) /ˈfrɪɡət/
helicopter (n) /ˈhelɪˌkɒptə(r)/
IFV (infantry fighting vehicle) (n) /ˌaɪefˈviː (ˌɪnfəntri ˈfaɪtɪŋ ˌviːəkl)/
jeep (n) /dʒiːp/
jet fighter (n) /ˈdʒet ˌfaɪtə(r)/
stealth bomber (n) /ˈstelθ ˌbɒmə(r)/
submarine (n) /ˈsʌbməˌriːn/
tank (n) /tæŋk/
transport aircraft (n) /ˈtrænspɔːt ˌeəkrɑːft/

Task 2 Write three words for each group.

military aircraft:	1 *stealth bomber*	2	3 ....
armoured vehicles:	4	5	6 ....
naval ships:	7	8	9 ....

Tank

Task 3 Translate.

armament (n) /ˈɑːməmənt/
commander (n) /kəˈmɑːndə(r)/
crew (n) /kruː/
driver (n) /ˈdraɪvə(r)/
gunner (n) /ˈɡʌnə(r)/
hull (n) /hʌl/

loader (n) /ˈləʊdə(r)/
machine gun (n) /məˈʃiːn ˌɡʌn/
main gun (n) /ˈmeɪn ˌɡʌn/
tracks (n) /træks/
turret (n) /ˈtʌrɪt/

Task 4 Tick the four members of a tank crew.

Gadgets

Task 5 Translate.

digital camera (n) /ˌdɪdʒɪtəl ˈkæm(ə)rə/
GPS receiver (global positioning system) (n) /dʒiːpiːˈes rɪˌsiːvə(r)/
lap top (n) /ˈlæp tɒp/
mobile phone (n) /ˌməʊbaɪl ˈfəʊn/
PDA (personal digital assistant / palm top computer) (n) /ˌpiːdiːˈeɪ/
SW radio (short wave) (n) /ˈreɪdiəʊ/

Task 6 Which gadgets can you put in your pocket or wear on your belt?

alpha

Task 1 Complete the sentences. Use *was* or *were*.

1 The first plane *was* flown by the Wright brothers in 1903.

2 The first atomic bomb .... exploded in New Mexico.

3 The rockets .... launched from the base this morning.

4 These ships .... built in Rotterdam.

5 Electricity .... discovered by Edison in the 19th century.

6 Compact discs .... invented in 1989.

Task 2 Complete the sentences. Use these verbs in the passive.

| use   lay   connect   discover   ~~invent~~ |

1 Telegraph was *invented* by Morse in 1837.

2 Universities were first .... to the Internet in 1969.

3 Buses were first .... as public transport in Britain in 1834.

4 The first version of the computer virus 'Friday 13th' was .... in 1987.

5 The first submarine cable was .... between Europe and America in 1866.

bravo

Task 1 Complete the sentences. Use *can* or *can't*.

1 Amphibious craft *can* move over land or on water, but they *can't* fly.

2 A submarine .... travel underwater.

3 A helicopter .... take off vertically, but it .... fly long distances.

4 Radar .... detect the stealth bomber.

5 An IFV .... protect infantry soldiers when they are fighting.

Task 2 Look at the chart and complete the sentences. Use *can* or *can't*.

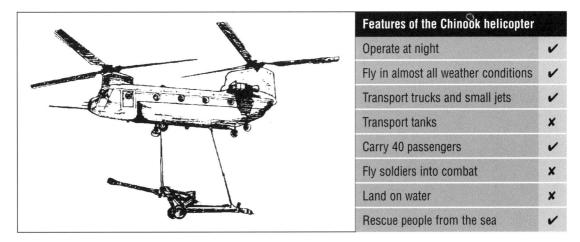

Features of the Chinook helicopter	
Operate at night	✔
Fly in almost all weather conditions	✔
Transport trucks and small jets	✔
Transport tanks	✘
Carry 40 passengers	✔
Fly soldiers into combat	✘
Land on water	✘
Rescue people from the sea	✔

1 The Chinook *can* operate at night.

2 It .... fly in almost all weather conditions.

3 It .... transport trucks and small jets, but it .... transport tanks.

4 It .... carry 40 passengers, but it .... fly soldiers into combat.

5 It .... land on water, but it .... rescue people from the sea.

charlie

Task 1 Read the text and complete the specifications.

Challenger 2 Main Battle Tank (MBT)

Challenger 2 is a main battle tank. It was developed for the British Army and has excellent battlefield mobility. It can travel across rough terrain at 40 kilometres per hour, and on roads it has a maximum speed of 56 km/h. The tank is fitted with Chobham armour and weighs 62,500 kilograms. It is 3.5 metres wide and 2.49 metres high. The approximate length of the tank is 8.33 metres. The main armament consists of a Royal Ordnance 120 mm gun called the L30 and when the gun is pointing forward, the tank has a length of 11.5 metres. It has a crew of four: the commander, the gunner, the loader and the driver.

Specifications

1   name of vehicle *Challenger 2 MBT*

2   armament ....

3   crew ....

4   maximum road speed .... km/h

5   height .... m

6   weight .... kg

7   width .... m

Task 2 Look at the specifications in Task 1 and write the questions.

1   How *much does it weigh*? It weighs 62,500 kilograms.

2   How .... ? It has a crew of four.

3   How .... ? It can travel at a maximum speed of 56 km/h.

4   How .... ? It's 2.49 metres high.

5   How .... ? It's 3.5 metres wide.

delta

Task 1 Read the programme and answer the questions.

At the end of the course …

1   Can they do basic first aid? *Yes, they can.*

2   Can they drive a tank? ....

3   Can they read maps? ....

4   Can they send smoke signals? ....

5   Can they use a compass? ....

> # Basic survival course
>
> – orienteering, compass, map work, first aid

Task 2 Match.

1   GPS   a   It can carry a section of soldiers.

2   IFV   b   It can fly at 602 km/h.

3   PDA   c   It can store and play music.

4   MP3 player   d   It can send e-mails.

5   C130   e   It can locate your position.

echo   Task 1 Complete the text. Use *can*, *could*, *can't* or *couldn't*.

Tanks

In the First World War, tanks (1) *couldn't* provide troops with much protection.

Before, tanks (2) .... only fire their main gun when they weren't moving.

Now they (3) .... fire and move at the same time.

In the Battle of Cambrai in 1917, tanks (4) .... move very fast – only about 5 kilometres per hour. Now they (5) .... travel at speeds of up to nearly 60 kilometres per hour on open roads. They (6) .... also travel over rough terrain, but they (7) .... manoeuvre very well in forests.

foxtrot   Task 1 Read and answer the questions about the Zeppelin.

The Zeppelin

The Zeppelin was a type of aircraft, built by Count Ferdinand von Zeppelin. The first Zeppelin, the LZ1, was tested on 2nd July 1900. The LZ1 could only fly at 28 kilometres per hour, but the LZ38 of 1915 had a maximum speed of 96 kilometres per hour.

The Zeppelin was made of aluminium and looked like a very fat cigar. It was designed for military use in almost any weather conditions. During the War, the Zeppelins operated at night. The target cities could be seen easily and the Zeppelins could return home before first light. At first the British pilots couldn't catch them because the Zeppelins could travel fast and they also carried many machine guns for protection. But then new planes were built with a powerful new weapon. This weapon could burn the hydrogen gas inside the Zeppelin. The days of the Zeppelin as a military front-line weapon were finished.

1   What type of transport was the Zeppelin? *A type of aircraft.*

2   Who built it? ....

3   When was it first tested? ....

4   What was it made of? ....

5   What did it look like? ....

6   Why couldn't the British pilots catch the Zeppelins at first?

    ....

7   How could the new weapon destroy the Zeppelin?

    ....

listening

Task 1 [30] 💿 **Listen and write the numbers.**

1   To convert inches into centimetres, multiply by ....

2   To convert feet into metres, multiply by ....

3   To convert miles into kilometres, multiply by ....

4   To convert nautical miles into kilometres, multiply by ....

5   To convert Centigrade into Fahrenheit, multiply by ...., divide by .... and add ....

Task 2 [31] 💿 **Listen and number the pictures.**

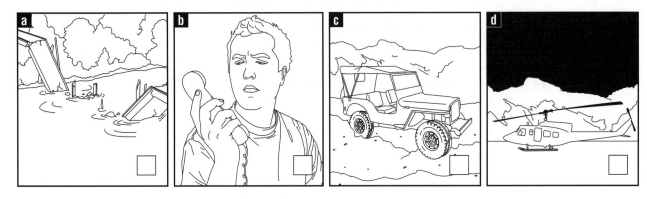

Task 3 [32] 💿 **Listen and write the specifications.**

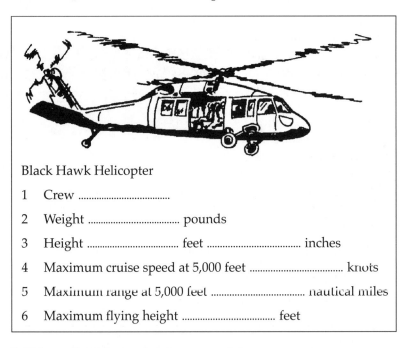

Black Hawk Helicopter

1   Crew ....

2   Weight .... pounds

3   Height .... feet .... inches

4   Maximum cruise speed at 5,000 feet .... knots

5   Maximum range at 5,000 feet .... nautical miles

6   Maximum flying height .... feet

Task 4 [33] 💿 **Listen and write true or false.**

1   The Black Hawk helicopter is manufactured in the USA, Japan and Korea. ....

2   It is designed to transport soldiers to the battlefield. ....

3   It can only be used to carry troops into battle. ....

4   It can't carry anti-armour missiles. ....

5   It can fly in almost all weather conditions. ....

6   Its communications system can identify friend or foe. ....

Review 1 (Units 1–7)

Task 1 Which word is different? Why?

Example: a zero   b two   c eight   ⓓ alpha *It isn't a number.*

	a		b		c		d	
1	Juliet		Mike		Patricia		Victor	
2	Pakistan		Algerian		Bosnian		American	
3	lunch		breakfast		dinner		coffee	
4	football		first aid		karate		swimming	
5	squad		cookhouse		barracks		mess	
6	quartermaster		major		medic		adjutant	

Task 2 Complete the series.

Example: one, two, three, *four*

1 nine, ten, ..., twelve

2 ...., X-ray, Yankee, Zulu

3 Monday, ..., Wednesday, Thursday

4 first, second, ..., fourth

5 lieutenant, captain, major, ...

6 sergeant, corporal, lance corporal, ...

Task 3 Complete the words.

Example: t _e_ n n _i_ s (a sport)

1 t _ _ t h p _ s t _ (a personal item)

2 c _ f f _ _ (a drink)

3 w _ _ p _ n s (training)

4 _ n g _ n _ _ r (a profession)

5 h _ l _ c _ p t _ r (transport)

6 n _ n _ t y - _ _ g h t (a number)

Task 4 Complete the sentences. Use *on, in, at* or *to*.

Example: The class is *on* Thursday.

1 The class is .... Monday morning.

2 The briefing is .... 0800 hours.

3 We start training .... the morning.

4 PT is from 1400 .... 1600 hours.

5 He was born .... 1965.

6 The flight is .... 21.15.

Task 5 Circle the correct word.

Example: He's *a*/ *an* French airman.

1 She is *a* / *an* Australian doctor.
2 Do you have *any* / *some* batteries?
3 We need *some* / *a* shoe polish.
4 There *isn't* / *aren't* any good maps.

5 They are *German* / *Germans* tanks.
6 I don't need *a* / *any* compass.
7 *Is* / *Are* there any people in the building?
8 We found *these* / *this* guns in the truck, sir.

Task 6 Circle the correct word.

Example: My name *is*/ *am* Major Thompson.

1 Good morning. I *am* / *is* Captain Boyd.
2 *Do* / *Does* it fire rounds?
3 Where *were* / *was* you born?
4 They *weren't* / *didn't* train for war.

5 She *runs* / *run* for her country.
6 He *cans* / *can* speak Russian and Polish.
7 *Were* / *Did* you posted abroad?

Task 7 Circle the correct word to complete the sentences.

Example:

I'd like .... batteries, please.
(a) some   b any   c a   d one

1 How .... are you staying?
  a long   b much   c old   d time

2 How .... does it weigh?
  a many   b tall   c much   d big

3 .... are you going?
  a Where   b Who   c Which   d What

4 What .... does the train arrive?
  a hour   b time   c long   d often

5 How .... does a ticket cost?
  a money   b quantity   c many   d much

Task 8 Complete the sentences. Use *a, an, the* or — (no word).

Example: He is *a* captain.

1 Do you play .... basketball?
2 Are you in .... navy?
3 She's .... interpreter.
4 He was promoted to the rank of .... airman first class.
5 There's .... restaurant on Station Road.
6 He works for .... UN.

Task 9 Write short answers.

Example: Are you in the army? Yes, I *am.*

1   Did you have a good flight? Yes, we ....

2   Can you understand this? No, I ....

3   Are they training? Yes, they ....

4   Does Sgt Minter know the plan? Yes, he ....

5   Is the situation under control? No, it ....

Task 10 Read. Then circle the correct answer.

> Alexander the Great was a Greek military leader. His father, Philip II, was a general and his teacher was Aristotle. When Alexander was only 18, he was a commander in his father's army and then he was ambassador in Athens. When he was 20 years old, his father was killed and Alexander became King of Macedonia.
>
> His country was often at war: Thebes, Tyre, Asia Minor, Persia, Afghanistan, India were all conquered by Alexander and his men. But Alexander wasn't killed in battle, he died from malaria in Babylon when he was only 33 years old.
>
> Alexander the Great was married and had one son. But Alexander died before the boy was born and the empire was divided into independent countries.

1   Alexander the Great was
   a   from Greece.
   b   a Roman emperor.
   c   a bad military leader.
   d   a commander in the Greek navy.

2   His father was
   a   Aristotle.
   b   a general.
   c   King of Greece.
   d   born in Afghanistan.

3   He was only .... when his father died.
   a   18.
   b   20.
   c   a young boy.
   d   33.

4   Alexander the Great
   a   was born in Babylon.
   b   died in Greece.
   c   was killed in battle.
   d   died when he was 33 years old.

5   Alexander had
   a   two wives.
   b   two sons.
   c   one child.
   d   one daughter.

The NATO school

glossary Military alliances

Task 1 Translate.

agreement (n) /əˈgriːmənt/ *An arrangement or decision about what to do.*
alliance (n) /əˈlaɪəns/ *A group of countries that agree to provide defence for each other.*
ally (allies) (n) /ˈælaɪ(z)/ *A friendly country, a member of an alliance.*
attack (vb) /əˈtæk/ *To start a fight.*
common interests (n) /ˌkɒmən ˈɪntrəsts/ *To have the same objectives.*
defence (n) /dɪˈfens/ *Actions taken to protect someone or something from attack.*
defend (vb) /dɪˈfend/ *To protect someone or something from attack.*
member of an organisation (n) /ˈmembə(r)/ *To be or become part of a group.*
negotiate (vb) /nɪˈgəʊʃiˌeɪt/ *To talk or discuss and reach an agreement.*
negotiations (n) /nɪˌgəʊʃiˈeɪʃnz/ *Talks or discussions to reach an agreement.*
partnership (n) /ˈpɑːtnəʃɪp/ *An alliance or agreement to work together.*
peace (n) /piːs/ *The opposite of war.*
peace-keeping forces (n) /ˈpiːskiːpɪŋ ˌfɔːsɪz/ *Troops that are placed between two opposing forces to stop them fighting and maintain the peace.*
peace-keeping operations (n) /ˈpiːsˌkiːpɪŋ ˌɒpəˈreɪʃnz/ *Missions or tasks designed to maintain peace.*
peace talks (n) /ˈpiːs tɔːks/ *Discussions to reach an agreement to stop fighting.*
self-defence (n) /ˌselfdɪˈfens/ *Protection of your own interests.*
sign (vb) /saɪn/ *To write your name.*
treaty (n) /ˈtriːti/ *An official or written agreement between two or more countries.*

Task 2 Complete the puzzle.

1 Countries sign this when they decide to help each other.
2 Talks or discussions to try to reach a solution
3 To write your name at the end of a document.
4 A group of countries that agree to defend one another.
5 A written agreement between countries.
6 A form of alliance to work together.
7 The objective of the United Nations for the whole world.
8 A country that is part of an international organisation.

alpha

Task 1 Answer the questions.

1 Where is Geneva?
   It's in the southwest.

2 Where is Biel?

   ....

3 Where is Zurich?

   ....

4 Where is Bellinzona?

   ....

5 Where is St Moritz?

   ....

Task 2 Complete the table. Use these words.

> Algerian   Sudanese   Swedish   Hungarian   Japanese   ~~Swiss~~
> Canadian   Israeli   Latvian   Indian   Turkish   Thai

A 1 syllable	B ● •	C ● ••	D •• ●	E • ● •	F • ● ••
Swiss					

bravo

Task 1 Complete the sentences. Use *all*, *most*, *some* or *a few*.

Requirements of delegates for the conference	
lunch	100%
accommodation	95%
translation service	85%
tourist information on city	42%
transport from airport	12%

1 *Some* delegates require tourist information on the city.

2 .... delegates require transport from the airport.

3 .... of them want lunch.

4 .... of them need a translation service.

5 Almost .... of them requested accommodation.

charlie

Task 1 Write the questions.

1 Where *are you going* (you go)?

2 How .... (you get) there?

3 When .... (you leave)?

4 How long .... (you go) for?

5 Where .... (you stay)?

Now match the questions to the answers.

a I'm going by plane. ☐   d I'm going to Helsinki. ☐1☐

b I'm staying at a four-star hotel. ☐   e I'm going on 6th June. ☐

c I'm going for four days. ☐

Task 2 Complete the sentences. Use *for, on, in* or *at.*

1 We're staying *at* the Hotel Excelsior *for* one week.

2 They're arriving .... 2000 hours.

3 Are you leaving .... Sunday?

4 We're staying there .... two hours.

5 We're having lunch .... ten minutes' time.

delta

Task 1 Answer the questions. Use these phrases.

| by sea   by road   by rail   ~~by air~~   on foot |

1 When you take a plane, how do you travel? *By air.*

2 When you take your car, how do you travel? ....

3 When you buy a ticket for the train, how do you travel? ....

4 When you go to Madeira by boat, how do you travel? ....

5 When you decide to walk somewhere, how do you travel? ....

Task 2 Put the conversation in order.

Passenger

a ☐1☐ Good morning.

b ☐   Thank you. How much is that?

c ☐   That's fine. I'd like a single to Geneva, please.

d ☐   And how long does the journey take?

e ☐3☐ What time is the next train to Geneva, please?

Railway clerk

f ☐2☐ Good morning.

g ☐   To Geneva? Er … The next train is at 10.45. There's one every hour.

h ☐   It takes one hour and twenty minutes. The 10.45 arrives in Geneva at 12.05.

i ☐   That's fourteen euros.

j ☐   A single to Geneva? Here you are.

echo   **Task 1** Complete.

The hotel is five minutes from the (1) *airport*. All rooms have a private
(2) .... , (3) .... , direct (4) .... line and
mini-bar. The hotel has a gym, a sauna and a large (5) ....
A breakfast buffet is served from 7 to 8.30 am, lunch from 12 to 2.30 pm and
evening meals from 7.30 pm until the (6) .... closes at 10.30 pm. Early
morning wake-up calls can be arranged. All (7) .... are accepted.

foxtrot   **Task 1** Complete. Use *could*, *let's* or *don't*.

1   Why *don't* we rent a car and go to the beach for the day?

2   We .... get the train to the coast and then go for a walk.

3   .... go swimming this afternoon.

4   Why .... we visit the villagers tomorrow?

5   We .... stop for a meal in the next town.

Task 2 Look at the weather in New Zealand and answer the questions.

1   What's the weather like
     in Auckland?
     It's sunny with southwest winds.
     The maximum temperature is
     17° C and the minimum is 10° C.

2   What's the weather like
     in Wellington?

     ....
     ....
     ....

3   What's the weather like
     in Christchurch?

     ....
     ....
     ....

4   What's the weather like
     in Dunedin?

     ....
     ....
     ....

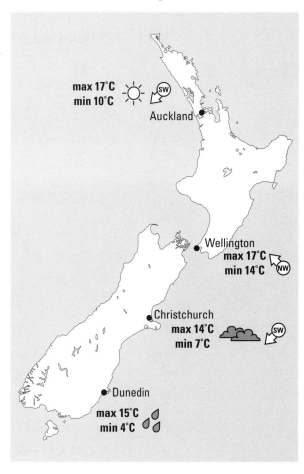

listening

Task 1 [34] 🔘 **Listen and complete the chart.**

	type of transport	time of departure	destination
1			
2			
3			

Task 2 [35] 🔘 **Listen and complete the agenda.**

Mon 10.00 Sec. Gen. from National Union

12.00 _____

13.30 _____ with local council

16.00 meeting with Chief of Police

17.30 _____ Miles

Tue

Task 3 [36] 🔘 **Listen and tick the correct picture.**

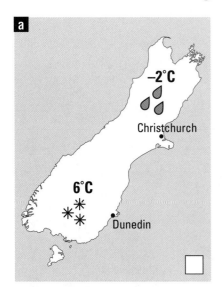

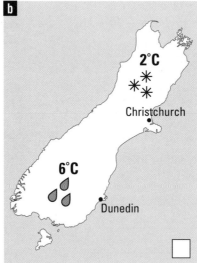

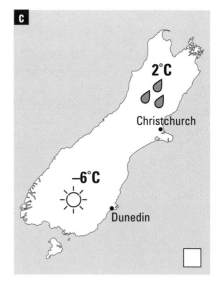

Task 4 [37] 🔘 **Listen and number the messages.**

a ☐ B5D wants permission to land.

b ☐ Convoy leaving tomorrow 0600, ETA 0830 hours.

c ☐ Staying at Hotel President room 38 – come for a drink.

d ☐ DESERT RAT meeting WZ at Black Lion – 8.30 pm.

Fit to fight

glossary   Health problems

Task 1 Translate.

ache (n) /eɪk/ *I need to see a dentist – I have terrible toothache.*
bite (n / v) /baɪt/ *He has lots of mosquito bites. / A dog bit him.*
blister (n) /ˈblɪstə(r)/ *My boots are too small – I have a big blister on my foot.*
broken arm (n) /ˌbrəʊkən ˈɑːm/ *She has a broken arm.*
bruise (n / v) /bruːz/ *He has a terrible bruise on his leg. / He bruised his leg.*
burn (n / v) /bɜːn/ *He has a burn on his hand. / He burnt his hand on the hot engine.*
casualty (n) /ˈkæʒuəlti/ *The casualties were taken to hospital.*
cold (n) /kəʊld/ *He caught a bad cold last winter.*
cough (n) /kɒf/ *He has a terrible cough – probably because he smokes too much!*
cut (n / v) /kʌt/ *She has a cut on her leg. / She cut herself on the wire.*
diarrhoea (n) /ˌdaɪəˈrɪə/ *The mayonnaise in that restaurant was bad and now he has diarrhoea.*
fever (n) /ˈfiːvə(r)/ *He had a fever all week. His temperature was 39° C at one point.*
headache (n) /ˈhedeɪk/ *I took some painkillers for my headache.*
heat exhaustion (n) /ˈhiːt ɪgˌzɔːstʃən/ *They were out in the midday sun and are now suffering from heat exhaustion.*
hypothermia (n) /ˌhaɪpəˈθɜːmiə/ *They are suffering from hypothermia after their night on the mountain.*
injury (n) /ˈɪndʒəri/ *He can't run because he has a leg injury.*
injure (v) /ˈɪndʒə(r)/ *He injured his leg in the gym.*
pain (n) /peɪn/ *He woke up in the middle of the night with terrible stomach pains.*
shock (n) /ʃɒk/ *After the accident, he was suffering from shock and couldn't speak.*
sprain (n / v) /spreɪn/ *He has an ankle sprain. / He fell over and sprained his ankle.*
wound (n / v) /wuːnd/ *He has a head wound. / He was wounded in the head.*

First aid

Task 2 Translate.

bandage (n) /ˈbændɪdʒ/
field dressing (n) /ˈfiːl ˌdresɪŋ/
painkiller (n) /ˈpeɪnkɪlə(r)/
plaster (n) /ˈplɑːstə(r)/
splint (n) /splɪnt/

Task 3 Match.

1	head wound	a	splint
2	broken arm	b	field dressing
3	blister	c	bandage
4	headache	d	plaster
5	leg injury	e	painkiller

alpha

Task 1 Write questions.

1 How *often do you do strength exercises*? I do strength exercises once a day.

2 How ....? I eat fast food every week.

3 How ....? I smoke about ten a day.

4 How ....? I'm twenty-six years old.

5 How ....? I weigh about 85 kilos, I think.

6 How ....? I'm about 1 metre 80.

Task 2 Write sentences.

1 aerobic exercises? (Three to five times a week). *He does aerobic exercises three or five times a week.*

2 smoke? (No) ....

3 eat fast food? (Never) ....

4 strength exercises? (About once a week) ....

5 age? (24) ....

6 weight? (79 kg) ....

Task 3 Make comparisons.

1 Herter | fit than | Smith *Herter is fitter than Smith.*

2 Smith | heavy than | Herter ....

3 Herter | muscular than | Smith ....

4 Herter | good than | Smith at push-ups ....

5 Smith | bad than | Herter on the assault course ....

bravo

Task 1 Complete the chart. Use these phrases.

> ~~smoke~~   watch TV all day   go for a walk
> relax   drive everywhere   go for a swim

It's bad for your health to …	It's good for your health to …
1 smoke	4 ....
2	5 ....
3	6 ....

Now write advice using *should* or *shouldn't*.

1 *It's bad for your health to smoke. You shouldn't smoke.*

2 ....

3 ....

4 ....

5 ....

6 ....

charlie

Task 1 Complete the sentences. Use these words.

| eat   dish   food   ~~meal~~   meat |

1 MRE means *Meal, Ready-to-Eat*.

2 Vegetarians do not eat ....

3 Fast .... is eaten all over the world.

4 *Ceviche* is a famous .... from Peru.

5 You should .... more fruit and vegetables.

Task 2 Complete the sentences with *more* or *less*.

1 The Japanese eat *more* fish than most people.

2 The British use .... olive oil in their cooking than the Spanish.

3 France produces .... wine than Ireland.

4 In Italy they make .... whisky than in Scotland.

5 In Mozambique they eat .... vegetables and cereals than meat.

delta

Task 1 Circle the correct answer.

1 What are chips / French fries?
   a fried potatoes   b boiled potatoes   c baked potatoes

2 What is sushi?
   a grilled fish   b boiled fish   c raw fish

3 What is Hungarian goulash?
   a a type of soup   b a type of vegetable   c a type of salad

4 What is paella?
   a a meal with pasta   b a meal with rice   c a meal with beans

5 What is Indian curry?
   a a sweet meal   b a salty meal of fish   c a hot and spicy meal

Task 2 Write polite requests using *could*.

1 You want to see the menu. *Could you bring me the menu, please?*

2 You want some more bread. ....

3 You want another cup of coffee. ....

4 You want the bill. ....

Task 3 Write requests using *can*.

1 You can't reach the salt. *Can you pass the salt, please?*

2 You want to have some more rice. ....

3 You can't reach the water. ....

4 You want white coffee. ....

echo

Task 1 Find two answers for each question.

1 Are you feeling better today? $\boxed{f}$ $\square$

2 What's the matter? What's wrong? $\square$ $\square$

3 Where's the pain exactly? $\square$ $\square$

4 Can you move it? $\square$ $\square$

a No, I can't. I think it's broken.
b I have a terrible headache.
c Yes, I can, but it's very difficult.
d In my right side.

e I have a very bad cough.
f Well, I'm less weak, but I can't walk.
g Right here in my neck.
h Yes, much better, thank you.

foxtrot

Task 1 Describe the procedures for a stomach wound. Use *must* or *mustn't*.

1 Do not touch the wound. *You mustn't touch the wound.*

2 Do not lie the casualty on their side. ....

3 Put the casualty's legs at 45°. ....

4 Apply a field dressing. ....

5 Do not give the patient any food. ....

Task 2 Match.

1 burn

2 cut

3 snake bite

a Clean the area with soap and stop the bleeding with a bandage.

b Cool the area and clean it with some soap. Do not give the patient anything to eat.

c Cool the area, and apply a field dressing. Give the patient some water to drink.

Task 3 Match.

1 arm $\boxed{f}$
2 chest $\square$
3 elbow $\square$
4 finger $\square$
5 foot $\square$
6 hand $\square$
7 head $\square$
8 knee $\square$
9 leg $\square$
10 neck $\square$
11 shoulder $\square$
12 stomach $\square$

listening

Task 1 [38] 🎧 **Listen and write the numbers.**

1 cans of peaches ....   5 jars of coffee ....

2 cans of pears ....   6 jars of honey ....

3 cans of tomatoes ....   7 jars of lentils ....

4 cans of beans ....   8 jars of black beans ....

Task 2 [39] 🎧 **Listen and tick the food on the menu.**

Menu

First course

Russian salad ☐

egg mayonnaise ☐

green salad ☐

French omelette ☐

green beans ☐

onion soup ☐

Main course

chicken and chips ☐

grilled ribs ☐

steak and chips ☐

salmon ☐

spaghetti Bolognese ☐

Irish stew ☐

Task 3 [40] 🎧 **Listen and tick the correct procedure.**

1 a Put the patient on their side. ☐

   b Lie the patient on their back. ☐

2 a Put a blanket over them. ☐

   b Do not cover them. ☐

3 a Give the patient something to eat. ☐

   b Give the patient something to drink. ☐

Task 4 [41, 42] 🎧 **Listen and complete the chart.**

	Request 1	Request 2
How many casualties are there?		
What is the problem?		
Where?		

Task 5 [43] 🎧 **Listen and number the problems.**

☐ mine victim

☐ hypothermia

☐ heat exhaustion

10 War games

glossary Terrain features

Task 1 Translate.

desert (n) /ˈdezət/ *A large area of land without trees or water and often covered with sand.*
draw (n) /drɔː/ *A small valley coming down the mountainside.*
ford (n) /fɔːd/ *A shallow part of a river. You can walk or drive across the river here.*
forest (n) /ˈfɒrɪst/ *A large area of land covered with trees and vegetation.*
grass (n) /grɑːs/ *A green plant found in fields and eaten by animals.*
hill (n) /hɪl/ *Similar to a mountain, but much smaller and lower.*
jungle (n) /ˈdʒʌŋgl/ *A tropical rainforest.*
lake (n) /leɪk/ *A large area of water surrounded by land.*
marsh (n) /mɑːʃ/ *An area of low, wet land.* (adjective: marshy /ˈmɑːʃi/)
mountain (n) /ˈmaʊntɪn/ *A mass of very high land going up to a peak.*
oasis (n) /əʊˈeɪsɪs/ *An area in a desert with trees and water.*
pass (n) /pɑːs/ *A narrow route through the mountains.*
ravine (n) /rəˈviːn/ *A very deep, narrow valley.*
ridge (n) /rɪdʒ/ *A long, narrow stretch of high land.*
river (n) /ˈrɪvə(r)/ *Water flowing naturally into the sea or a lake.*
saddle (n) /ˈsædl/ *A ridge rising at each end to a high point.*
sand dune (n) /ˈsændjuːn/ *A ridge of sand formed by the wind.*
scrub (n) /skrʌb/ *Land covered with small trees and bushes.*
spur (n) /spɜː(r)/ *A ridge extending from a hill or a mountain.*
valley (n) /ˈvæli/ *The land between mountains or hills, often with a river flowing through it.*
wood (n) /wʊd/ *An area of land covered with trees; smaller than a forest.*

Task 2 Write three places for these uniforms.

desert camouflage uniform

1 *desert*   2 ....   3 ....

woodland / jungle camouflage uniform

4 ....   5 ....   6 ....

alpha

Task 1 Match.

1   A multinational exercise   a   is an exercise for marines to practise landing on enemy beaches.

2   A joint exercise   b   is an exercise to practise command and communications with computers.

3   A Field Training Exercise (FTX)   c   is an exercise with troops from many different countries.

4   A Command Post Exercise (CPX)   d   is an exercise to practise military skills in a realistic operation.

5   An airborne assault   e   is an exercise with ground forces, air forces and naval forces.

6   An amphibious assault   f   is an exercise for parachutists to practise jumping behind enemy lines.

Task 2 Complete. Use *a, an, the* or — .

Bright Star is (1) *a* joint exercise. It is (2) .... important part of combat training.

Servicemen and women from (3) .... army, navy and air force participate in

(4) .... exercise. It takes place in (5) .... north-east of Egypt, near

(6) .... Mediterranean. (7) .... troops all practise military skills.

(8) .... marines carry out amphibious assaults and (9) .... parachutists

carry out airborne assaults. (10) .... special command post is established to

practise command and communications with (11) .... computers.

Task 3 Add *the* where necessary.

1   *The* General is ready to see you, ma'am.

2   .... United Arab Emirates borders on .... Red Sea.

3   Peruvians celebrate .... Festival of .... Sun in .... June.

4   .... headquarters of .... Red Cross is in Geneva, in .... Switzerland.

5   .... hottest part of the country is in .... south.

bravo

Task 1 Circle the correct answers.

1   Which is the biggest?   ⓐ an ocean   b a sea   c a lake

2   Which is the driest?   a an oasis   b a desert   c a marsh

3   Which is the largest?   a a town   b a village   c a city

4   Which is the deepest?   a a ravine   b a ditch   c a valley

5   Which is the most difficult for a tank? a snow   b desert   c a marsh

Task 2 Write the superlative of the adjectives in brackets.

1   The *highest* (high) mountain in Europe is in Switzerland.

2   Holland is one of the .... (flat) countries in the world.

3   This is one of the .... (hilly) parts of the country.

4   This is one of the .... (wide) routes through the mountains.

5   The .... (wet) part of Ireland is over in the west.

charlie

Task 1 Match these terrain features with the numbers on the map.

marsh ☐   ravine ☐   ridge ☐   flat land ☐   hill 1

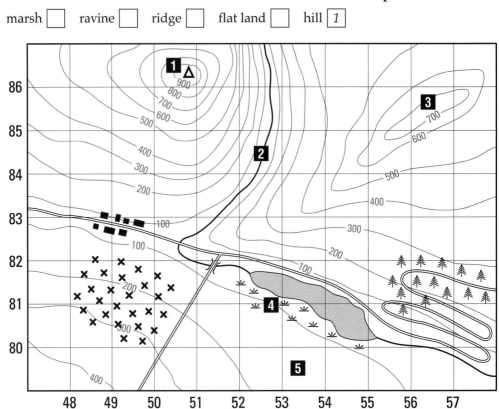

Now write true or false.

1   There's a bridge at grid 513819. *true*

2   There's a lake between grid 523818 and grid 552802. ....

3   There's a minefield between grid 523818 and grid 552802. ....

4   There's a village at grid 532810. ....

5   There's a hill at grid 508863. ....

delta

Task 1 Complete with the opposite adjective.

1   The city's really ugly. It isn't very *beautiful.*

2   The town is really dirty. It isn't very ....

3   The place is really boring. It isn't very ....

4   The airport is really old. It isn't very ....

5   This street is really noisy. It isn't very ....

Task 2 Match.

1   What's the city like?   a   Well … it isn't cheap!

2   Can you recommend a hotel?   b   The city? Oh, it's really exciting.

3   What's the weather like?   c   Oh, it's very lively at night.

4   Do you know any good clubs?   d   It's very cold in winter.

5   What's the nightlife like?   e   Yes, the Abraxas disco is very popular.

6   Is it very expensive?   f   Yes, you should stay at the Western.

echo

Task 1 Complete the sentences. Use these words.

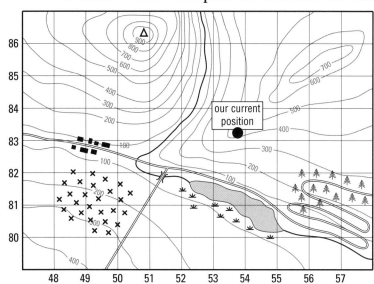

| in   on top of   between   over   ~~round~~ |

1 There's a road *round* the lake.

2 There's a radio antenna .... the hill.

3 There's a bridge .... the river at grid 513819.

4 There's a ridge .... grid 555849 and grid 573859.

5 There's a wood .... the vicinity of grid 570815.

Task 2 Look at the map. Write the direction.

1 There's a road junction about 2 km *southwest* of here.

2 There's a village 4 km .... of our current location.

3 The ridge is about 2 or 3 km .... of our current location.

4 We can see an antenna on a hilltop about 4 or 5 km .... of our current position.

5 The wood begins about 2½ km .... of here.

6 The lake is less than 2 km .... of our current location.

Task 3 Match.

1	Enemy HQ	a	is at grid 674798.
2	Some friendly forces	b	is moving in the vicinity of the wood.
3	There's a landing zone	c	is about 100 m south of the border.
4	A column of tanks	d	are located 5 km north of the river.
5	Our recce platoon's current location	e	200 m west of our current position.

foxtrot

Task 1 Complete the sentences. Use these words.

| attack   check   evacuate   ~~land~~   move   provide   remain |

1 1st Platoon will *land* first and secure the landing zone.

2 3rd Pl will .... from here to the assembly area on foot.

3 A recce party will .... the area east of the landing zone.

4 A Company will .... the enemy position on the left flank.

5 B Company will .... cover on the right flank.

6 C Company will .... in a defensive position in the rear area.

7 A helicopter will .... the casualties.

listening

Task 1 [44] 💿 **Listen and complete the orders.**

First platoon will deploy in firing positions at grid (1) ....

Second platoon will assault the position from the (2) ....

Third platoon will remain in reserve position 100 m to the (3) .... of the LZ.

Task 2 [45] 💿 **Listen and write the locations.**

1 the communications centre ....   4 some friendly forces ....

2 an enemy tank ....   5 current location ....

3 a minefield ....

Task 3 [46] 💿 **Listen and mark the pilot's position.**

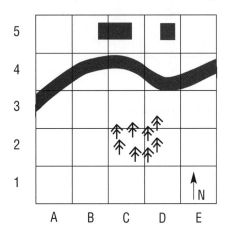

Task 4 [47] 💿 **Listen and mark the minefields on the map.**

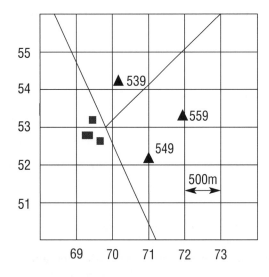

Task 5 [48] 💿 **Listen and complete the landing zone report.**

1	**Surface of LZ area:** *grass*	**4**	**Landmarks:**
2	**Location:**	**5**	**Obstacles:**
3	**Distance from the nearest village:**	**6**	**Direction of wind:**

Peacekeeping

glossary Peacekeeping

Task 1 Translate.

buffer zone (n) /ˈbʌfə ˌzəʊn/ *An area of separation between enemy forces or countries.*

ceasefire (n) /ˈsiːsfaɪə(r)/ *A temporary agreement to stop fighting.*

conflict (n) /ˈkɒnflɪkt/ *A serious disagreement or difference of opinion.*

demining (n) /diːˈmaɪnɪŋ/ *The process of clearing a minefield.*

demobilise (v) /diːˈməʊbəˌlaɪz/ *To make a soldier a civilian again.*

disarm (v) /dɪsˈɑːm/ *To take away a person's weapons.*

elections (n) /ɪˈlekʃnz/ *The formal process of choosing someone for political office.*

humanitarian missions (n) /hjuːˌmænɪˈteəriən ˈmɪʃnz/ *These operations help the local population in times of great difficulty or need. For example, they provide food, medical treatment or shelter.*

monitor (v) /ˈmɒnɪtə(r)/ *To observe and control an agreement, a ceasefire, elections, etc.*

NGO (n) /ˌendʒiːˈəʊ/ *Non-Governmental Organisation. Its mission is to help people in times of difficulty or need.*

patrol (v) /pəˈtrəʊl/ *To observe and control an area.*

peacekeeper (n) /ˈpiːskiːpə(r)/ *A soldier sent by the UN to help maintain a truce between countries or communities.*

peacekeeping operations (n) /ˌpiːskiːpɪŋ ɒpəˈreɪʃnz/ *These missions are conducted by neutral military or civilian personnel to protect a truce or to help refugees return to their homes.*

protection force (n) /prəˈtekʃn ˌfɔːs/ *These soldiers are sent to defend the local population from attack.*

refugee (n) /ˌrefjuˈdʒiː/ *A person without a home as a result of a military conflict.*

supervise (v) /ˈsupəvaɪz/ *To control or monitor a situation.*

truce (n) /truːs/ *A permanent agreement to stop fighting.*

UNMOs (n) /ˈʌnməʊz/ *United Nations Military Observers. These soldiers are sent to supervise after a conflict.*

Task 2 Complete with words from the glossary.

1   An agreement to stop fighting: *truce* or ....

2   To take someone's weapons or stop them being a soldier: .... or

    ....

3   To control a situation: .... or ....

4   Soldiers can't be deployed in this place: ....

5   These military personnel are sent to control the situation after a conflict:

    .... or ....

Task 3 Write these out in full.

1   UN   *United Nations*

2   NGO   ....

3   UNMO ....

alpha

Task 1 Read and answer the questions.

The Office of the United Nations High Commissioner for Human Rights

'The mission of the Office of the United Nations High Commissioner for Human Rights (OHCHR) is to protect and promote all human rights for all.'

Mission statement, Geneva, 2000

The post of the High Commissioner was created in 1993 to report to the Secretary General of the United Nations on the situation of people's civil, cultural, economic, political and social rights all over the world, based on the Universal Declaration of Human Rights, signed on 10th December 1948.

The Office of the UN High Commissioner works together with governments, international and regional organisations, NGO's and civilians to monitor how countries meet their obligations on human rights and to produce agreements. It is the moral authority of the United Nations and acts as a 'voice for victims' and an alarm bell for the world community.

The Office of the United Nations High Commissioner for Human Rights is located in Geneva, Switzerland. There is also a second office in the building of the UN HQ in New York.

---

1 Who is responsible for human rights at the United Nations?

The Office of the High Commissioner for Human Rights (OHCHR).

2 When was the post of High Commissioner for this assignment created?

....

3 Who does the UN High Commissioner report to?

....

4 What does the OHCHR monitor?

....

5 Where is the High Commissioner's office?

....

bravo

Task 1 Complete. Use *about*, *so* or *like*.

1 Oh, yes. I think *so*.

2 No, I don't think ....

3 And what .... the situation outside the capital?

4 What is the situation .... outside the capital?

Task 2 Match.

1	What was the mission like?	a	It was a very dangerous place.
2	What was it like in 1990?	b	Yes, I think so.
3	Do you think the mission was successful?	c	Well, we're still clearing them.
4	What is it like today?	d	I think it was successful.
5	What about the landmines?	e	Oh, it's much safer now.

charlie

Task 1 Complete. Use *Always* or *Never*.

> ### Code of conduct
> 1 *Always* respect other people's rights.
> 2 .... respect the environment of the host country.
> 3 .... react emotionally to one side in the conflict.
> 4 .... be punctual.
> 5 .... drink alcohol when you're on duty.

Task 2 Complete the puzzle. Use these words.

> tolerant   patient   environment   neutral   ~~respect~~   opinions   host   fair   code

1 *Respect* people's rights and opinions.
2 .... of conduct.
3 We should respect people's rights to have different ....
4 Respect the laws, culture and religion of the .... country.
5 Be .... Treat all people the same.
6 Be .... Don't support any of the sides in the conflict.
7 Be .... Wait, and don't complain.
8 Respect the .... of the host country.
9 Be .... Respect all people's rights and opinions.

Crossword:
1 R E S P E C T
2 E
3 N
4 S
5 I
6 T
7 I
8 V
9 E

delta

Task 1 Complete with the opposite adjective. Use these words.

> reserved   cold   ~~rude~~   lazy

1 He isn't very polite. I think he's very *rude*.
2 He isn't very hardworking. I think he's very ....
3 He isn't very friendly. I think he's very ....
4 They aren't very open. I think they're very ....

Task 2 Circle the correct phrase.

1 A (Excuse me.)/ *Thank you*. I'm sorry to interrupt.
  B What is it?
2 A I'm really sorry.
  B *You're welcome. / That's OK.*
3 A We're getting married!
  B *Congratulations! / I'm sorry!*
4 A Quiet, *thank you. / please.*
  B Sorry.

echo

Task 1 Match.

1	Sappers	a	Military mine clearance.
2	A safe lane	b	Soldiers with special training in mine clearance.
3	Breaching	c	Humanitarian mine clearance.
4	A minefield	d	A path clear of mines.
5	Demining	e	An area with mines.

Task 2 Match.

1 Why is safety more important than speed for humanitarian deminers? $\boxed{b}$

2 Why is speed important in breaching a minefield? $\boxed{}$

3 Why must humanitarian deminers clear all the mines from an area? $\boxed{}$

4 Why don't sappers clear all the mines in a minefield? $\boxed{}$

a Because their objective is only to make a safe lane.
b Because they must clear all the mines for civilians to return home.
c Because it is often done under enemy fire.
d Because it must be safe for civilians to live there.

foxtrot

Task 1 Match the words with the pictures. Then complete the sentences.

body armour $\boxed{c}$ metal detector $\boxed{}$ mines $\boxed{}$ prodder $\boxed{}$

red triangle $\boxed{}$ trip wires $\boxed{}$ visor $\boxed{}$

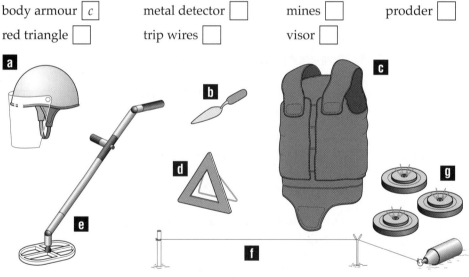

Before he starts work, the deminer puts on (1) *body armour* and a (2) ....

First of all, the deminer studies the terrain, checks for (3) .... and clears the vegetation.

Next, he checks the terrain with a (4) ....

Then, he checks with a (5) .... where the metal detector located metal.

When he finds a mine, he marks the place with a (6) ....

Finally, all (7) .... are destroyed at the end of the day.

Task 2 Underline the sequencing words or phrases in Task 1.

listening

Task 1 [49] 🔊 **Listen and number.**

☐ Coy   ☐ Col   ☐ Capt   ☐ km   ☐ Cpl

Task 2 [50] 🔊 **Listen and write the acronyms.**

1 ....

2 ....

3 ....

4 ....

5 ....

Task 3 [51] 🔊 **Listen and write the number.**

1 Schools open. *400*

2 Phones connected in villages. ....

3 Refugees returning by plane. ....

4 Homes destroyed. ....

5 Banks open. ....

6 UN police officers recruited. ....

Task 4 [52] 🔊 **Listen and tick the duties the peacekeeper talks about.**

1 checking the buffer zone   ☐

2 supervising elections   ☐

3 clearing mines   ☐

4 disarming soldiers   ☐

5 helping refugees go home   ☐

6 providing medical support   ☐

Task 5 [53] 🔊 **Listen and number.**

Rules of Engagement

a ☐ Be ready to defend yourself and your unit.

b ☐ Only open fire if you come under attack.

c ☐ Treat all people with respect.

d ☐ All military operations should be conducted according to the laws of war.

e ☐ Use the minimum force to carry out the mission.

f ☐ Only detain civilians for security reasons or in self-defence.

glossary HQ

Task 1 Translate.

briefing room (n) /ˈbriːfɪŋ rʊm/ *The room for giving and receiving information or instructions.*
cell (n) /sel/ *The smallest structural and functional unit of an organisation.*
chief of staff (n) /ˌtʃiːfəvˈstɑːf/ *This person is responsible for the running of a headquarters.*
compound (n) /ˈkɒmpaʊnd/ *An area with a fence around it.*
CO's office (n) /siːˈəʊzˌɒfɪs/ *The room where the Commanding Officer works.*
headquarters (n) /ˈhedkwɔːtə(r)z/ HQ /eɪtʃˈkjuː/ *The place occupied by a military commander and his staff.*
information management (n) /ɪnfəˈmeɪʃn ˌmænɪdʒmənt/ *The organisation or administration of specific information or data.*
movement control detachment (n) /ˌmuːvmənt kənˈtrəʊl dɪˌtætʃmənt/ *The department cell responsible for controlling movement of personnel and supplies.*
Ops room (n) /ˈɒps rʊm/ *The operations room.*
personnel (n) /pɜːsəˈnel/ *The workers or employees.*
registry (n) /ˈredʒɪstri/ *The place where records and files are kept.*
restricted area (n) /rɪˌstrɪktɪd ˈeəriə/ *Only people with permission are allowed in this area.*
Secretary General (n) /ˌsekrətri ˈdʒenrəl/ *The person in charge or responsible for an organisation.*
sector (n) /ˈsektə(r)/ *A branch or part of an organisation.*
staff officer (n) /ˈstɑːf ˌɒfɪsə(r)/ *This person is in charge of a cell.*
subordinate (n) /səˈbɔːdɪnət/ *A person with a lower rank.*
superior (n) /suːˈpɪəriə(r)/ *A person with a higher rank.*

Task 2 Write:

| three rooms. | 1 *briefing room* | 2 .... | 3 .... |
| three jobs. | 4 .... | 5 .... | 6 .... |

Security measures

Task 3 Translate.

alert state (n) /əˈlɜːt ˌsteɪt/ *Level of possible danger: green = normal, yellow = higher level of security, red = high risk.*
authorisation (n) /ˌɔːθəraɪˈzeɪʃn/ *Official permission to do something.*
barbed wire (n) /ˌbɑːbd ˈwaɪə(r)/ *Wire with short, sharp points used for fences.*
barrier (n) /ˈbærɪə(r)/ *A wall or fence to control movement and provide protection.*
chain of command (n) /ˌtʃeɪn əv kəˈmɑːnd/ *Military orders pass through this sequence of ranks.*
co-ordination (n) /kəʊˌɔːdɪˈneɪʃn/ *The process of organising people or things to make them work together effectively.*
sandbag (n) /ˈsændˌbæg/ *A bag filled with sand to use as a defence.*
sangar (n) /ˈsæŋgə/ *A small protective structure built up from the ground to observe or fire from.*
searchlights (n) /ˈsɜːtʃˌlaɪts/ *Powerful lights to discover movement in the area.*
sentry (n) /ˈsentri/ *A soldier posted to keep watch and guard a building.*
tank stops (n) /ˈtæŋk ˌstɒps/ *Obstacles placed in the road to prevent or stop tanks from passing.*

Task 4 Write three types of barrier.

1 *barbed wire*   2 ....   3 ....

alpha

Task 1 Complete the sentences. Use *for, of, to* or *by*.

1 The Head of Mission reports *to* the UN Secretary General in New York.

2 The Secretary General is responsible .... all UN peacekeeping operations and reports .... the UN Security Council.

3 The Force Commander is in charge .... the military component and is responsible .... the HOM.

4 Each area of operation is under the command .... a Sector Commander.

5 Each AO has a sector HQ, support elements and two or three infantry battalions commanded .... contingent commanders.

Task 2 Complete the chart. Use these words.

> Head of Mission   Force Commander   ~~UN Secretary General~~   Sector Commander

United Nations Security Council
1   *Un Secretary General*
2 ....
3 ....
4 ....
Contingent Commander

bravo

Task 1 Circle seven words connected with rifles.

A	R	O	U	N	D	S	L
Q	L	S	J	H	T	L	M
C	O	I	W	Z	R	I	P
M	A	G	A	Z	I	N	E
B	D	H	D	E	G	G	G
O	K	T	N	P	G	V	T
L	F	S	O	K	E	M	B
T	V	B	A	R	R	E	L

1 *rounds*
2 m...................................
3 b...................................
4 l...................................
5 s...................................
6 t...................................
7 s...................................
8 b...................................

Task 2 Circle the correct word.

1 You aren't *prohibited* / *allowed* to load or unload weapons inside a building.

2 You are *prohibited* / *permitted* to carry weapons only when you are on duty.

3 It is *permitted* / *prohibited* to carry loaded weapons onto a civilian aircraft.

4 You are not *allowed* / *prohibited* to carry your rifle in the 'load' position.

5 It is not *prohibited* / *permitted* to leave your weapon unattended.

charlie

Task 1 Complete the telephone conversation. Use these phrases.

> That's correct   I read back   Good evening   Hold on   ~~say your name and rank~~

A   Good evening, Ops Room.

B   Good evening. I'd like to speak to the duty officer, please.

A   Please (1) *say your name and rank*.

B   I'm Captain Robertson from HQ Ops Room.

A   (2) .... , please.

C   Hello, duty officer.

B   (3) .... This is Captain Robertson at HQ Ops Room.
    I'm calling to inform you the alert state will change to green at 2400 tonight.

C   (4) .... The alert state will change to green at 2400.

B   (5) ....

Task 2 Complete the telephone conversation. Use these words.

> call   give   ~~speak~~   be   say

A   Good morning, Ops Room.

B   This is Lt Boyne from movement control. Can I (1) *speak* to Sergeant Hawkins, please?

A   Please (2) .... again.

B   Yes. This is Lt Boyne from movement control. Can you (3) .... me Sergeant Hawkins, please?

A   I'm sorry, Sergeant Hawkins isn't in the office. He'll (4) .... back at 11.00.

B   OK. I'll (5) .... back. Thank you.

A   Thank you, goodbye.

delta

Task 1 Make the orders more polite.

1   Bring me the report. *Could you bring me the report?*

2   Give him a message. ....

3   Tell me the time. ....

4   Show me where the major's office is. ....

5   Drive us back to HQ. ....

6   Make me a copy of this. ....

Task 2 Match.

1   Can you sign here?   a   order

2   Could you sign here, please?   b   request

3   Sign here.   c   polite request

echo

Task 1 Complete the sentences. Use these words.

> barbed wire   car park   sangar   ~~searchlights~~   sentry   tank stops

1   There are *searchlights* on the roof of the main building.
2   There's a .... made of sandbags at every corner of the building.
3   There's a .... fence around the compound.
4   There's a .... for visitors outside the compound.
5   There's a .... on duty 24 hours a day.
6   There are .... in front of the barrier at the main entrance.

Task 2 Complete the sentences.

> ~~in front of~~   outside   round   inside   at

1   There are tank stops *in front of* the barrier.
2   There is a car park .... the compound and another one for visitors outside.
3   There is a checkpoint .... the main gate.
4   We have a sentry .... the main building.
5   There are defence positions .... the compound.

foxtrot

Task 1 Write the names of the rooms.

1   The Ops room is the first door on the left.
2   The registry is opposite the Ops Room.
3   The CO's office is at the end of the corridor on the left.
4   The briefing room is the third door on the right, at the end of the corridor.
5   S1 is next to the Ops Room – the second door on the left.
6   The bathroom is between the Registry and the briefing room – down the corridor on the right.

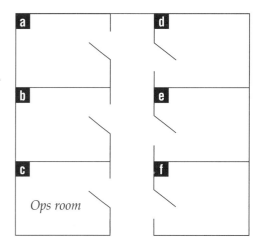

Task 2 Order the conversation.

a   ☐   Pete: Yes, I think so. What time does it start?
b   ☐   Marco: At 11.30. But come half an hour earlier so you have time to change.
c   ☐   Pete: Sure. I'd love to. Where are we playing?
d   ☐   Marco: There's a basketball game next Saturday morning against the local team. Do you want to come?
e   ☐   Marco: At the local ball park. Do you know where it is?

listening

Task 1 [54] 🔘 **Listen and tick the correct message.**

1

- dinner in Officers' Mess
- Tues @ 6pm
- dress uniform

☐

2

- dinner in Sergeants' Mess
- Thursday at 8 o'clock
- informal dress

☐

3

- dinner in Sergeants' Mess
- Tuesday at 20.00 hrs
- dress uniform

☐

Task 2 [55, 56, 57] 🔘 **Listen and write the messages.**

1

MESSAGE

From:

To:

Message:

2

MESSAGE

From:

To:

Message:

3

MESSAGE

From:

To:

Message:

Task 3 [58] 🔘 **Listen and write the telephone numbers.**

1 ....

2 ....

3 ....

Task 4 [59] 🔘 **Listen and complete.**

> CAMP ORDERS
> - *WEAPONS* Weapons should be carried at (1) .... in the (2) '....................'
>   position.
> - *COMMANDER'S BRIEF* Commander's brief is at (3) .... Monday to
>   (4) .... [day] and at 1800 on (5) .... [day].
> - *DRESS* (6) .... uniform should be worn at all times on the camp.
> - *ALCOHOL* For security, alcohol is (7) .... on the camp.
> - *WORK PARTIES* There will be work parties on (8) .... [day], Wednesday and
>   (9) .... [day] from (10) .... to 1200.

Task 5 [60] 🔘 **Listen and write *R* for request or *O* for order.**

1 ☐   2 ☐   3 ☐   4 ☐   5 ☐

Convoy

glossary Convoy

Task 1 Translate.

convoy (n) /ˈkɒnvɔɪ/ *A group of vehicles travelling together and escorted by the military for protection.*

distance (n) /ˈdɪstəns/ *The space between two things or two people.*

escort (n) /ˈeskɔːt/ *A person, vehicle, ship or aircraft that accompanies for protection or security, or to show respect.*

escort (v) /esˈkɔːt/ *To accompany for protection or security.*

overtake (v) /ˌəʊvəˈteɪk/ *To pass another vehicle travelling in the same direction.*

release point (RP) (n) /rɪˈliːs ˌpɔɪnt (aːˈpiː)/ *The place where the convoy commander releases control of the convoy.*

repair (v) /rɪˈpeə(r)/ *To fix or mend something that is damaged.*

reporting point (n) /rɪˈpɔːtɪŋ ˌpɔɪnt/ *A place on a route where vehicles report.*

route (n) /ruːt/ *A way to reach a destination from a specific start point.*

start point (SP) /ˈstɑːt pɔɪnt (esˈpiː)/ *The place from where a convoy starts.*

Task 2 Label the diagram.

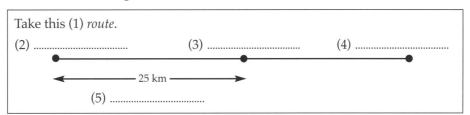

Take this (1) *route.*

(2) ....   (3) ....   (4) ....

← ———— 25 km ————→

(5) ....

Roads

Task 3 Translate.

checkpoint (n) /ˈtʃekˌpɔɪnt/ *A barrier at a border. Security checks are carried out at this place.*

crossroads (n) /ˈkrɒsˌrəʊdz/ *An intersection of two roads.*

curve (n) /kɜːv/ *The road is not straight here.*

exit (n) /ˈeksɪt/ *Traffic can leave a motorway, main road or roundabout here.*

junction (n) /ˈdʒʌŋkʃn/ *The place where two or more roads, rivers or railway lines meet.*

rest area (n) /ˈrest ˌeəriə/ *A place to stop and relax.*

roadblock (n) /ˈrəʊdˌblɒk/ *A barrier on a road to stop and check the traffic.*

roadworks (n) /ˈrəʊdˌwɜːks/ *The road is being repaired here.*

roundabout (n) /ˈraʊndəˌbaʊt/ *A junction with several exits where all the traffic moves in the same direction.*

signpost (n) /ˈsaɪnˌpəʊst/ *At a road junction, this gives the direction and distance to a place.*

speed limit (n) /ˈspiːd ˌlɪmɪt/ *The maximum speed permitted on a specific road.*

traffic lights (n) /ˈtræfɪk ˌlaɪts/ *Three lights – red, amber and green – that control traffic at junctions.*

Task 4 Make words.

area	block	~~check~~
lights	limit	~~point~~
post	rest	road
sign	speed	traffic

1 check point

2 ....

3 ....

4 ....

5 ....

6 ....

alpha

Task 1 Match.

1. The convoy will set off
2. They will complete a radio check
3. They will stop for 20 minutes
4. The trucks will report
5. The convoy commander will hand over control

a. when they reach the first rest area.
b. when they get to each checkpoint.
c. when the medical supplies arrive.
d. when they leave the start point.
e. when the convoy finally reaches the release point.

bravo

Task 1 Read. Then write the letters.

☐ start point   ☐ reporting point   ☐ release point

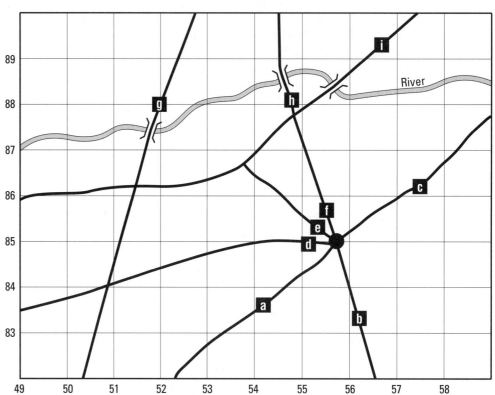

Your start point is the service station on the A2, marked on your map at grid 562 832. You link up with the humanitarian aid convoy here at 0600 and take the A2 north. The A2 is a main road but remember that the convoy's trucks are slow and so your maximum speed will be 40 km/h.

Continue along the A2 until you reach the roundabout. Take the third exit at the roundabout. This exit is signposted B23. Your reporting point and rest area are on the B23, just after the roundabout.

When you leave the rest area, drive along the B23 until you come to a T-junction. Turn left at the junction and take the B25 until you get to the crossroads. Turn right and continue along the B26 (signposted Frip) for about twenty kilometres until you come to a bridge across the river. Cross the bridge and continue for two kilometres. Your release point is the hospital immediately on your left as you enter Frip. Your ETA at Frip hospital is 0845.

charlie

Task 1 Use the verbs in brackets to complete the sentences.

1 *Send* for medical support if anyone *is* injured. (send, be)

2 .... very slowly if there .... any road works. (drive, be)

3 .... the map if you .... not sure of the route. (check, be)

4 .... for help if you .... not repair the vehicle. (call, can)

5 Don't .... your vehicle if it .... stopped at a checkpoint. (leave, be)

Task 2 Match.

1 If your vehicle breaks down,   a stop and change the wheel.

2 If you see a traffic accident,   b stay with the vehicle and send a SITREP to the control station.

3 If your vehicle has a flat tyre,

4 If you are stopped at a checkpoint, c drive fast and leave the area.

5 If the convoy is ambushed,   d give first aid and call for a medic.

                                       e move to the side of the road and report to the control station.

delta

Task 1 Complete the crossword.

¹E			²			³T		⁴W
		⁵B		⁶T		⁷S		
⁸I		⁹		¹⁰R			¹¹R	
	¹²W							
¹³L			¹⁴K		¹⁵		¹⁶	
				¹⁷L	¹⁸		¹⁹	
	²⁰L							

ACROSS

3 If your car breaks down, you .... it to a garage.

5 In American English, this part of a car is called a *trunk*, and in British English?

7 The abbreviation for *southwest*.

8 They got .... a taxi.

9 They got .... a bus.

10 Convoys do this at the reporting point.

12 In British English, it's the big window at the front of a vehicle, and in American English?

13 The opposite of *right*.

17 The maximum speed you can travel on a specific road.

20 For traffic, these are red, amber and green.

DOWN

1 A place where traffic can leave a motorway, main road or roundabout.

2 A 10-.............. truck.

3 A dual carriageway has .... lanes in each direction.

4 The opposite of *dry*.

5 In American English, this part of the car is called the *hood*, and in British English?

6 Another word for *lorry*.

7 The tank's maximum road .... is 56 km/h.

11 If you don't have a car, you can .... one from a company.

12 Most cars have four of these and a spare one, plus one for steering!

14 Carry a repair .... in case the vehicle breaks down.

15 I .... your driver.

16 Turn left .... the crossroads.

18 We're going .... the car.

19 At the checkpoint you can show your driving licence or military ....

Task 2 Complete the conversation. Use these phrases.

> Just three days, please.   ~~I'd like to rent a car, please.~~   Here you are.
> I'm sure that will be fine.   I'm not going far.

Attendant:	Good afternoon. Can I help you?
Mr Dupont:	Yes, (1) *I'd like to rent a car, please.*
Attendant:	Yes, what kind of car would you like, sir?
Mr Dupont:	Not very big – (2) ....
Attendant:	Well, we have an economy model at 65 euros a day including insurance.
Mr Dupont:	Yes, (3) ....
Attendant:	Very good, sir. How many days do you want to rent the vehicle for?
Mr Dupont:	Er … (4) ....
Attendant:	Three days … that's fine. Could I see your driving licence, please?
Mr Dupont:	Yes, of course. (5) ....

echo

Task 1 Match.

1	The antenna (aerial) is moving.	a	He needs to replace it.
2	The tyre is flat.	b	He needs a jack.
3	The headlight is damaged.	c	He needs to charge it.
4	The petrol tank is empty.	d	He needs a screwdriver.
5	The battery is flat.	e	He needs to fill it up.
6	The spare wheel is needed.	f	He needs to fill it up with air.

foxtrot

Task 1 Match the prowords with the definitions.

> say again   roger   read back   out   closing down   over   ~~I say again~~

1 I'm repeating my message. *I say again.*

2 I received your message. ....

3 This is the end of my transmission. I don't expect a reply. ....

4 I'm stopped and I'm getting out of the vehicle. I won't be in radio contact. ....

5 This is the end of my transmission. I'm waiting for your reply. ....

6 Read the message back to me. ....

7 Repeat your message. ....

listening

Task 1 [61] 🔊 Listen and tick the correct convoy.

1 ◀ | APC | T | APC | T | T | APC | APC | T | T |

2 ◀ | APC | T | T | APC | T | T | T | APC | APC |

3 ◀ | APC | T | T | T | APC | APC | T | T | APC |

Task 2 [62] 🔊 Listen and circle the correct information.

CONVOY COMMANDER'S BRIEFING	
DATE:	2nd (1) *June / July*
MISSION:	escort (2) *UN / military* convoy from KALE to DORF
	ETD: 0700 ETA: (3) *1115 / 1150*
route	**directions**
A5	Take the A5 (4) *east / west*.
B35	Junction with B35. Take the (5) *first / third* exit at the roundabout. The exit is signposted B35.
B33	Junction with B33. Turn left at the junction and take the B33. Continue along the B33 for (6) *13 / 30* kilometres until you come to the first reporting point at the bridge. Cross the bridge. The rest area is the service station on your left.

Task 3 [63] 🔊 Listen and mark the reporting points – O1, O2 and O3 on the map.

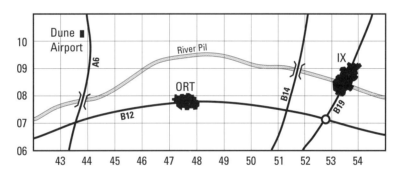

[63] 🔊 Listen again and write the ETA.

1   O1   2   O2   3   O3   4   IX ....

Task 4 [64, 65, 66, 67] 🔊 Listen and complete.

1   A   Hello D1, this is R3. (1) .... Over.

    B   D1. (2) .... Over.

    A   R3. OK. (3) ....

2   A   Hello D1, this is R3. Leaving Z1 in (4) .... Now Mobile from Z1. Over.

    B   D1. (5) .... Out.

3   A   Hello D1, this is R3. (6) .... for thirty minutes at Z2. Over.

    B   D1. Roger. Out.

4   A   Hello D1, this is R3. (7) .... from Z2 (8) .... Z3. Over.

    B   D1. Roger. Out.

glossary Equipment

Task 1 Translate.

camo face cream (n) /ˌkæməʊ ˈfeɪs kriːm/ *A cream applied to the face to provide appropriate camouflage.*

flak jacket (n) /ˈflæk ˌdʒækɪt/ *A jacket made of heavy material with metal inside to protect against gunfire.*

folding shovel (n) /ˌfəʊldɪŋ ˈʃʌvl/ *A tool used for moving soil, snow or sand or other material by hand.*

holster (n) /ˈhəʊlstə(r)/ *A container for a pistol.*

kevlar helmet (n) /ˌkevlə ˈhelmɪt/ *A bullet-proof hat for the military.*

knife /naɪf/, fork /fɔːk/ and spoon /spuːn/ *Utensils for eating food.*

map case (n) /ˈmæp ˌkeɪs/ *A container for maps.*

mess tins (n) /ˈmes ˌtɪnz/ *Metal dishes with folding handles used by soldiers for cooking, eating and drinking.*

patrol pack (n) /pəˈtrəʊl ˌpæk/ *A small rucksack containing essential items – water, rations, first aid and ammunition.*

pouch (n) /paʊtʃ/ *A small bag usually attached to the belt or kept in a pocket e.g. ammunition pouch.*

rucksack (n) /ˈrʌksæk/ *A soldier's bag (carried on the back).*

sleeping bag (n) /ˈsliːpɪŋ ˌbæg/ *A warm bag to sleep in especially when camping outdoors.*

sleepmat (n) /ˈsliːp ˌmæt/ *A mat placed under the body to sleep on (instead of a bed).*

stove (n) /stəʊv/ *A portable cooker to heat rations or boil water on.*

torch (n) /tɔːtʃ/ *A portable light using batteries to see in the dark.*

water bottle /ˈwɔːtə ˌbɒtl/ and cup /kʌp/ *A container for water with a receptacle to drink it in.*

waterproof notebook (n) /ˈwɔːtəpruːf ˈnəʊtbʊk/ *A block of paper resistant to water.*

webbing (n) /ˈwebɪŋ/ *The system of belts, straps and pouches in the soldier's combat equipment.*

whistle (n) /ˈwɪsl/ *A small instrument used to make a sound given as a signal.*

Task 2 Tick the kit you take on patrol.

alpha

Task 1 Complete the sentences. Use these verbs.

| check   conduct   ~~observe~~   set up   prevent |

1   The patrol is tasked to *observe* and report all activities in the area.
2   The patrol's task is to .... a roadblock near the bridge.
3   Their mission is to .... a house search.
4   The patrol's mission was to .... an attack on the building.
5   Their task was to .... all vehicles on that road.

Task 2 Complete the text. Use these words.

| had   mission   order   ~~task~~   tasked |

A56's (1) *task* was to patrol the border. They (2) .... to conduct a recce of the area and report any hostile activity. Their (3) .... was to prevent the smuggling of weapons. They were (4) .... to stop all cars and check the passengers' documents. They were also given the (5) .... to search the local houses if they suspected anything strange.

bravo

Task 1 Match.

1   You must give a challenge   a   if they want to surrender.
2   Do not fire more rounds   b   only if you come under attack.
3   Deadly force is not authorised   c   before you open fire.
4   Do not attack enemy troops   d   unless your life is in immediate danger.
5   Open fire   e   than necessary.

Task 2 Complete the sentences. Use these prepositions.

| in   ~~against~~   at   under   on |

1   Never open fire *against* a crowd.
2   Only open fire if your life is .... immediate danger.
3   Only open fire if you come .... attack.
4   Do not mount an attack .... that hill.
5   Shoot straight .... the target.

charlie

Task 1 Complete the sentences. Use these words.

> shouting   cheering   ~~throwing~~   looting

1   It looks like some of the crowd are *throwing* stones.

2   It looks like some people are .... the shops.

3   The people look happy. They seem to be ....

4   These people seem hostile. They seem to be ....

Task 2 Complete the information. Use these sentences.

> It's probably about six or seven in the evening.   It looks like a demonstration.
> ~~There seem to be five or six people.~~   They all seem to be wearing jeans and T-shirts.
> They seem to be in the main street.   It looks like they're throwing stones.

S = Size (how many?) (1) *There seem to be five or six people.*

A = Activity (what's happening?) (2) ....

L = Location (where?) (3) ....

U = Unit (military: uniform? civilian: clothes?) (4) ....

T = Time (when?) (5) ....

E = Equipment (type of vehicles / weapons used?) (6) ....

delta

Task 1 Write the questions.

1   *What is the man like?* He looks very serious.

2   .... ? He's over-weight, with grey hair and a moustache.

3   .... ? He's about 50.

4   .... ? He's medium-height.

Now write sentences about the woman.

Character (5) ....

Appearance (6) ....

Height (7) ....

Age (8) ....

Task 2 Write the questions.

1   Which *man do the police want to question?*   They want to question <u>the man with the moustache</u>.

2   Which .... ? <u>That man</u> wants to make a phone call.

3   Which .... ? He knows <u>that woman</u>.

4   Who .... ? <u>The woman</u> lives in the area.

5   Who .... ? She looks like <u>the suspect</u>.

echo

Task 1 Write the sentences.

1 The | 40-litre | carrying | a | patrol | soldier | pack. | is
The soldier is carrying a 40-litre patrol pack.

2 UN | wearing | blue | they | berets? | Are

....

3 waterproof? | face cream | Is | that | camo

....

4 brown | I | a | small | have | case. | leather

....

5 is | Swiss | This | old | a | wonderful | knife.

....

6 in | right | is | corner. | the | bottom | It

....

foxtrot

Task 1 Match.

1	affirmative	a	I have a question.
2	negative	b	I have a message for you.
3	question	c	Go ahead!
4	send	d	I have your message and I will comply.
5	message	e	Yes/Correct.
6	acknowledge	f	No/Incorrect.
7	wilco	g	Say you understand.

Task 2 Order the conversation.

a [ ] T4. Send. Over.

b [ ] T4. Wilco. Over.

c [1] D3. Message. Over.

d [ ] D3. Roger. Over and out.

e [ ] D3. Reporting movement of hostile elements in the area. Request reinforcements. Over.

f [ ] D3. Affirmative. Send helicopters to LZ at Grid 356092. Over.

g [ ] T4. Question. Do you require helicopters? Over.

listening

Task 1 [68] 💿 **Listen and tick the correct person.**

Task 2 [69] 💿 **Listen and tick the correct column.**

RULES OF ENGAGEMENT (ROE)		
Deadly force	**Authorised**	**Not authorised**
1 If lives are in immediate danger.		
2 To stop <u>all</u> persons crossing the bridge.		
3 If a person threatens you with a deadly weapon.		
4 Against any civilian vehicle that doesn't stop at a checkpoint.		

Task 3 [70] 💿 **Listen and tick the items you hear.**

☐ flak jacket   ☐ sleepmat   ☐ water bottles

☐ stove   ☐ knife   ☐ sleeping bags

☐ mess tins   ☐ torch   ☐ ammo pouch

Task 4 [71] 💿 **Listen and complete.**

date	6th June
time	2125 hours
caller	(1) ....
message	(2) .... fire at grid (3) .... on
	(4) .... Main Street / Sea Road
	(5) .... injured (6) .... dead
request	(7) ....
action	Ambulance sent immediately to area

Review 2 (Units 8–14)

Task 1 Which word is different? Why?

Example: a Monday b Saturday ⓒ March d Wednesday
It isn't a day.

	a		b		c		d	
1	a	wilco	b	roger	c	under	d	over
2	a	signpost	b	traffic lights	c	crossroads	d	checkpoint
3	a	trip wires	b	red triangle	c	prodder	d	metal detector
4	a	wheel	b	bonnet	c	track	d	windscreen
5	a	restricted area	b	compound	c	registry	d	chain of command
6	a	saddle	b	ridge	c	valley	d	fog
7	a	painkillers	b	blister	c	burn	d	bite
8	a	trigger	b	book	c	barrel	d	magazine

Task 2 Write the colours.

Example: a London bus *red*

1 a UN peacekeeper's beret ....
2 the alert state between high risk and normal at a military base ....
3 a jungle camouflage uniform? .... and ....
4 the triangle to tell people there is an accident or breakdown on the road ....
5 the Dutch flag .... , ... and ....

Task 3 Circle the opposite word.

Example: black ⓐ white b grey

1	start point	a	reporting point	b	release point
2	negative (*radio language*)	a	positive	b	affirmative
3	ally	a	friend	b	enemy
4	land	a	take off	b	overtake
5	return ticket	a	single ticket	b	simple ticket
6	load (*your weapon*)	a	lock	b	unload

Task 4 Circle the correct form.

Example: You are not *allowed to*/ *permitted* smoke in here.

1 They were tasked *to recce* / *with recce* the perimeter.
2 Vehicles *can't* / *are not permitted* to use this road after 10 pm.
3 Their mission was *for to* / *to* defend the bridge.
4 Helicopters are *not allowed* / *shouldn't* to land on this roof.
5 It's *prohibited to* / *necessary* park here.

Task 5 Circle the correct word.

Example: The rescue party searched *at /(in)/ on / for* the mountains.

1 They travelled *at / in / on / for* convoy.
2 They waited *at / in / on / for* a message.
3 Their lives were not *at / in / on / for* immediate danger.
4 There were sandbags *at / in / on / for* the main entrance.
5 There are tanks moving *at / in / on / for* our right flank.
6 You are responsible *of / for / with / to* planning our route.
7 The troops will report *of / at / with / to* the Polish general.
8 The helicopter arrived *over / in / at / to* the landing zone early.
9 There's a sniper *on / in / for / to* the roof.
10 There is a fence *round / through / for / over* the perimeter.

Task 6 Complete the sentences with the correct form of the adjectives (comparative or superlative).

Example: This point is the *most important* (important).

1 This road is .... (safe) than the route along the coast.
2 This is the .... (deep) ravine in the area.
3 It's .... (windy) on the south than the north side.
4 The ground is .... (wet) over there than up by the forest.
5 This is the .... (difficult) place to land.
6 The .... (bad) area is in the mountains.

Task 7 Complete the sentences. Use these words.

after before if unless until when

Example: Continue along this road *until* you get to the roundabout.

1 First you must check for trip wires .... you prod the ground for mines.
2 Radio your base .... you need help.
3 Do not leave the camp .... last light. You could be shot in the dark by mistake.
4 Do not use deadly fire .... you are attacked and your life is in danger.
5 .... you reach the junction, turn left.

Task 8 Match the questions and answers.

1 What does he look like?   a He's fine, thank you.
2 What's he like?   b He loves going for long walks
3 How's your father?   c He's very tall with long, dark hair.
4 What does he like most?   d He's running round the base.
5 How does the patient seem?   e He's very hostile.
6 What's he doing?   f I think he looks better now.

Task 9 Write short answers.

Example: Are you in the Army? Yes, I *am*.

1   Should we go into the village? No, you ....

2   Will the patrol be out there all night? No, it ....

3   Was Lt Knight in charge of the first aid post? Yes, he ....

4   Did they receive the message? No, they ....

5   Were there any minefields in the area? Yes, there ....

Task 10 Read. Then choose the correct answer.

> The United Nations building is located in east Manhattan, New York. This area is an international zone, with its own security force, fire department and post service. (You can send postcards to friends at home with a special UN stamp!)
>
> The UN Headquarters consists of four main buildings. The fourth building – the Dag Hammarskjold Library – was added in 1961 at the southwest corner and is used by UN staff, delegations from member states and members of various missions. The General Assembly Hall is the largest room at HQ. More than 1,800 people can sit inside to discuss international problems and work for peace and treaties between nations.
>
> On the eastern side of the main entrance, there is a beautiful blue window, designed by Marc Chagall. Visitors can also see the Japanese Peace Bell inside its typical Japanese house made of wood. This was given to the UN by Japan in 1954 and is made from coins collected by children from 60 different countries.
>
> Outside, along First Avenue, you can see a display of flags of many different colours – one for each member state. They are placed in alphabetical order (in English!). So the first flag is for Afghanistan and the last one represents Zimbabwe.

1   The UN building is located
  a   east of Manhattan.
  b   on the east side of Manhattan.
  c   in four buildings.
  d   inside the Dag Hammarskjold Library.

2   The UN library can be used by
  a   all visitors.
  b   tourists.
  c   UN employees only.
  d   only a few people, including UN staff.

3   Marc Chagall's window is
  a   opposite the east entrance.
  b   next to the Japanese Bell.
  c   in the southwest corner.
  d   on one side of the main entrance.

4   The Japanese Peace Bella
  a   was made of wood.
  b   was made by children.
  c   was made from coins.
  d   was made by 60 different countries.

5   Which country has its flag at the UN nearest to the one from Afghanistan?
  a   India.
  b   USA.
  c   Pakistan.
  d   Argentina.

Answer key

Unit 1

glossary

Task 2

vehicles: armoured personnel carrier, infantry fighting vehicle, jeep, tank truck
aircraft: helicopter, plane

Task 4

Q	K	M	B	D	C	W	O
S	A	I	L	O	R	E	F
O	I	P	Z	C	J	K	F
L	R	A	B	T	D	F	I
D	M	U	V	O	W	F	C
I	A	N	M	R	I	S	E
E	N	G	I	N	E	E	R
R	P	Q	S	R	Y	X	W

alpha

Task 1

2 'm   3 're   4 're   5 's

Task 2

2 's   3 's   4 're, 're   5 'm

Task 3

1 I'm   2 meet   3 name

bravo

Task 1

2 British   3 American   4 French
5 Pakistani   6 Algerian

Task 2

2 isn't   3 'm not   4 aren't   5 aren't

charlie

Task 1

2 engineer   3 airman   4 journalist
5 soldier

Task 2

2 No, he isn't.
3 No, he isn't.
4 Yes, she is.
5 Yes, he is.

Task 3

2 an   3 a   4 a   5 an

delta

Task 1

2 Fine thanks, and you?
3 I'm very well, thanks.
4 How is your family?
5 They're very well, thank you.

Task 2

2 tomorrow   3 weekend
4 next week

echo

Task 1

2 Her, She's, She's   3 Her, She's, Her
4 His, He's, He's

Task 2

2 What's his job?
3 Where's he from?
4 What's his address?
5 What's his telephone number?
6 What's his e-mail address?

foxtrot

Task 1

two, three, four, five, six, seven, eight, nine, ten, eleven, twelve, thirteen, fourteen, fifteen, sixteen, seventeen, eighteen, nineteen, twenty

Task 2

2 six   3 four   4 one   5 three

listening

Task 1

1 d   2 e   3 j   4 z   5 u

Task 2

1 an IFV   2 the UN   3 the USA
4 CNN   5 an APC

Task 3

1 Excuse me, are you Mary Smith?
2 No, I'm not. That's Mary over there.
3 Oh, I'm sorry. What's your name?
4 Barbara. Barbara Stevens.
5 Where are you from, Barbara?
6 Me? I'm from London. Are you American?
7 No, I'm not. I'm from Canada.

Task 5

1 4 jeeps
2 3 IFVs
3 13 tanks
4 1 helicopter
5 2 trucks
6 2 APCs

Task 6

1 morning   2 Danzig   3 sailor
4 navy   5 19

Task 7

1 Liz Evans
2 The Grand Hotel, London Road
3 616 893542
4 Journalist

Unit 2

glossary

Task 2

communications training, field training, NBC training, weapons training

alpha

Task 1

2 train   3 sleep   4 go   5 teach

Task 2

2 don't wear   3 don't do   4 don't go

Task 3

1 Delta   2 Hotel   3 Lima   4 Papa
5 Tango   6 Zulu

Task 4

2 romeo five zero   3 charlie papa lima
4 alpha two delta   5 oscar nine zero

bravo

Task 1

3 Yes, they do.
4 No, they don't.
5 Yes, they do.

Task 2

2 e   3 a   4 c   5 b

charlie

Task 1

2 toothbrushes   3 maps
4 compasses   5 padlocks
6 countries

Task 2

24 – twenty-four		27 – twenty-seven
36 – thirty-six		42 – forty-two
45 – forty-five		54 – fifty-four
59 – fifty-nine		63 – sixty-three
72 – seventy-two		89 – eighty-nine
95 – ninety-five		98 – ninety-eight

delta

Task 1

1 U 2 C 3 C 4 U 5 U 6 C
3 a toothbrush 4 some toothpaste
5 some soap 6 a towel

Task 2

3 a 4 any 5 any 6 a 7 any 8 a

Task 3

3 How much is the radio?
4 How much are the batteries?
5 How much are the padlocks?
6 How much is the deodorant?

echo

Task 1

2 Where 3 When 4 What 5 What

Task 2

2 What time does he have breakfast?
   He has breakfast at half past six.
3 What time does he start training?
   He starts training at quarter past
   seven.
4 What time does he eat lunch?
   He eats lunch at twenty past twelve.

foxtrot

Task 1

2 zero six hundred hours
3 twenty-one hundred hours
4 twenty hundred hours
5 zero seven hundred hours

Task 2

2 on 3 at 4 on 5 at 6 at, on

Task 3

2 No, he doesn't. 3 Yes, he does.
4 No, he doesn't. 5 Yes, he does.

listening

Task 1

1 NB7 (November Bravo Seven)
2 DR40 (Delta Romeo Four Zero)
3 31AF (Three One Alpha Foxtrot)
4 OT125 (Oscar Tango One Two Five)
5 J50 (Juliet Five Zero)

Task 2

1 d 2 b 3 c 4 a

Task 3

1 1300 2 1330 3 1640 4 1700
5 1800 6 2030 7 2030 8 2200

Task 4

1 ✔ 2 ✗ 3 ✗ 4 ✗ 5 ✗ 6 ✔

Task 5

Reveille   0600
Breakfast   0615–0645
Training   0720–1210
Lunch   1220–1320

Unit 3

glossary

Task 2

to be deployed, to be posted, to be
promoted, to be transferred

Task 4

beret, cap, helmet

alpha

Task 1

2 Che Guevara was an Argentinian
   revolutionary. He was born in 1928
   and he died in 1967.
3 Erich Hartmann was a German pilot.
   He was born in 1922 and he died in
   1995.

Task 2

2 weren't, were 3 wasn't, was

bravo

Task 1

1 1542 2 1605

2 His full name was Jalal ud din
   Mohammed Akbar Ghazi.
3 He was the Emperor of India from
   1556 to 1605.
5 He was 63 years old when he died.

Task 2

2 Yes, he was.   3 Yes, it was.
4 No, he wasn't.   5 No, there weren't.

charlie

Task 1

2 entered 3 served 4 graduated
5 attended

Task 2

2 didn't enter 3 didn't serve
4 didn't graduate 5 didn't attend

delta

Task 1

2 Did you have a good meal at the
   restaurant?
3 Did Hamsa go to Hakim's wedding?
4 Did Martin and Steve play for the
   Rockets?
5 Did you stay at home yesterday?

Task 2

2 How did Hassim celebrate his
   birthday?
3 What time did José and his friends
   leave last Saturday?
4 What did your mother and father do
   yesterday?
5 Where did you go last night?

Task 3

2 is, is 3 P, is 4 P, is, is

echo

Task 1

2 Joe didn't wear a uniform.
3 They didn't follow the orders.
4 The NCO didn't salute the colonel.
5 We didn't do our exercises.

Task 2

2 wore 3 go 4 do 5 gave

foxtrot

Task 1

(Possible answers)
belt: polish
jacket: wash, clean, iron, brush
badge of rank: polish
trousers: wash, clean, iron, brush
beret: clean, brush

Task 2

2 made, had 3 put, went
4 did, drank 5 left

Task 3

2 Yes, they did.
3 No, they didn't.
4 No, they didn't.
5 Yes, they did.

listening

Task 1

/t/   worked, marched, stopped,
       finished
/d/   trained, served, died
/ɪd/   started, celebrated

Task 2

1 birthday 2 party 3 club

Task 3

1 ✔ 2 ✔ 3 ✗ 4 ✗ 5 ✔ 6 ✗

Task 4

Name   Paul Blackmore
Date of birth   13th November 1983
Place of birth New York
Marital status Married
Children   1 boy, 3 years old

Task 5

1 Sacramento 2 Glendale
3 Niagara 4 1992 5 Happy

Unit 4

glossary

Task 2

2 brigadier general 3 OF–3
4 Lt Col

Task 4

2 corps, division, brigade
3 brigade, regiment, battalion

alpha

Task 1

2 Lieutenant   3 Lieutenant Colonel
4 Lance Corporal   5 Captain
6 Sergeant

Task 2

2 sergeant   3 major   4 captain
5 lieutenant colonel

Task 3

3 b   4 e   5 a   6 c   7 f

bravo

Task 1

2 st   3 rd   4 th   5 th   6 th

Task 2

2 squad   3 lieutenant   4 platoon
5 second   6 battery   7 troops
8 company
key word: squadron

charlie

Task 1

2 sir   3 sir   4 Corporal
5 Private Thomson

delta

Task 1

2 d   3 a   4 b

Task 2

2 What   3 did   4 are   5 Is   6 do

Task 3

2 for   3 at, in   4 in

echo

Task 1

2 d   3 b   4 a

Task 2

2 fly   3 attack   4 command
5 collect   6 transport   7 provide

foxtrot

Task 1

2 There are between 8 and 12 soldiers
   in a squad in the US army.
3 There are between 30 and 40 soldiers
   in a platoon.
4 There are between 100 and 200
   soldiers in a company.
5 There are about 730 soldiers in a
   battalion.
6 There are between 236 and 313
   officers in a brigade.
7 There are about 16,000 NCOs and
   soldiers in a division.

Task 2

2 company   3 battalion   4 brigade
5 division   6 cavalry

listening

Task 1

1 d   2 c   3 a   4 b   5 e

Task 2

1st Armoured Brigade
2nd Cavalry Regiment
18th Airborne Corps
5th Infantry Division
3rd Signal Regiment
14th Artillery Regiment

Task 3

1 2nd December   2 09.30
3 3rd December   4 17.00
5 5th December   6 11.15

Task 4

1 Infantry   2 Engineers   3 Signal
4 Medical

Unit 5

glossary

Task 2

basketball, football, golf, table-tennis,
tennis, volleyball

Task 4

2 go down   3 go over   4 go under
5 go through   6 go across

alpha

Task 1

2 doing   3 practising   4 running
5 swimming   6 playing

bravo

Task 1

3 Yes, they are.
4 Yes, she is.
5 Yes, he is.
6 No, they aren't. They're playing
   volleyball.

charlie

Task 1

2 shorts   3 trainers   4 bat
5 sports bag   6 tracksuit   7 trainers
8 racket   9 caps

delta

Task 1

2 likes, doesn't mind
3 doesn't mind, doesn't like
4 doesn't like

Task 2

2 Yes, he does.
3 No, he doesn't.
4 No, he doesn't

echo

Task 1

2 We play golf once a week.
3 I do weight-lifting every morning.
4 They often go to the gym.
5 He never does sit-ups.

Task 2

2 are playing   3 climb   4 run
5 are practising

foxtrot

Task 1

2 c up, down   3 e under   4 a into
5 d through   6 b over

listening

Task 1

picture b

Task 2

sit-ups: 30 mins a day
weight-lifting: 30 mins a day
basketball: sometimes
volleyball: sometimes
swimming: once or twice a week
running: often, in the morning
table-tennis: sometimes

Task 3

1 c   2 f   3 a   4 e   5 b   6 d

Task 4

1 false   2 true   3 true   4 false
5 true

Unit 6

glossary

Task 2

2 In the Officers' Mess.
3 On the parade ground / square.

Task 4

2 The signals officer.
3 The company commander.

alpha

Task 1

3 adjutant   4 guard   5 guard
6 adjutant   7 guard

Task 2

2 taxi   3 time   4 weather   5 base

1 b   2 e   3 a   4 d   5 c

bravo

Task 1

1 this   2 that   3 These   4 those
5 here   6 that

charlie

Task 1

2 on   3 on, to   4 with   5 of
6 to, in

Task 2

2 inspected   3 provided   4 equipped
5 commanded   6 organised

Task 3

2 The troops are assigned to the UN.
3 I was promoted to sergeant after
  two years.
4 The regiment is stationed in
  Germany.

Task 4

2 Three: two anti-tank and one
  LBH squadron.
3 Lynx mark 7 and Gazelle.
4 The TOW missile system.
5 For reconnaissance missions.

delta

Task 1

A = Indian restaurant
B = supermarket
C = pharmacy
D = cinema
E = leisure centre
F = Italian restaurant
G = police station

Task 2

1 true   2 false   3 false   4 true
5 true

echo

Task 1

2 minefields   3 airfields
4 Amphibious   5 Parachute

foxtrot

Task 1

2 d   3 f   4 b   5 a   6 c

listening

Task 1

1 b   2 e   3 d   4 f   5 a   6 c

Task 2

1 false   2 true   3 false   4 true
5 true   6 false

Task 3

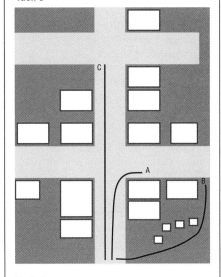

Task 4

1 P   2 N   3 P   4 P   5 N   6 N

Unit 7

glossary

Task 2

military aircraft: helicopter, bomber, jet
fighter, transport aircraft

armoured vehicles: APC, IFV, tank

naval ships: aircraft carrier, destroyer,
frigate, submarine

Task 4

commander, driver, gunner, loader

Task 6

mobile phone, GPS receiver, digital
camera, PDA

alpha

Task 1

2 was   3 were   4 were   5 was
6 were

Task 2

2 connected   3 used   4 discovered
5 laid

bravo

Task 1

2 can   3 can't   4 can't   5 can

Task 2

2 can   3 can, can't   4 can, can't
5 can't, can

charlie

Task 1

2 L30 (Royal Ordnance 120 mm gun)
3 four
4 56 km/h
5 2.49 m
6 62,500 kg
7 3.5 m

Task 2

2 How many crew does it have?
3 How fast can it travel?
4 How high is it?
5 How wide is it?

delta

Task 1

2 No, they can't.
3 Yes, they can.
4 No, they can't.
5 Yes, they can.

Task 2

2 a   3 d   4 c   5 b

echo

Task 1

2 could   3 can   4 couldn't   5 can
6 can   7 can't

foxtrot

Task 1

2 Count Ferdinand von Zeppelin.
3 On 2nd July 1900.
4 Aluminium.
5 A very fat cigar.
6 Because the Zeppelins could travel
  fast and they also carried many
  machine guns for protection.
7 It could burn the hydrogen gas
  inside the Zeppelin.

listening

Task 1

1 2.54   2 0.3048   3 1.609   4 1.852
5 9, 5, 32

Task 2

1 d   2 a   3 b   4 c

Task 3

1 3   2 11,780 pounds
3 16 feet 9 inches   4 162 knots
5 304 nautical miles   6 19,000 feet

Task 4

1 true   2 true   3 false   4 false
5 true   6 true

Review 1

Task 1

1 c Patricia. It isn't in the military alphabet.
2 a Pakistan. It isn't a nationality.
3 d coffee. It isn't a meal.
4 b first aid. It isn't a sport.
5 a squad. It isn't a place on a military base.
6 b major. It isn't a post, it's a military rank.

Task 2

1 eleven 2 Whisky 3 Tuesday
4 third 5 lieutenant colonel
6 private

Task 3

1 toothpaste 2 coffee 3 weapons
4 engineer 5 helicopter
6 ninety-eight

Task 4

1 on 2 at 3 in 4 to 5 in 6 at

Task 5

1 an 2 any 3 some 4 aren't
5 German 6 a 7 Are 8 these

Task 6

1 am 2 Does 3 were 4 didn't
5 runs 6 can 7 Were

Task 7

1 a 2 c 3 a 4 b 5 d

Task 8

1 — 2 the 3 an 4 — 5 a 6 the

Task 9

1 did 2 can't 3 are 4 does
5 isn't

Task 10

1 a 2 b 3 b 4 d 5 c

Unit 8

glossary

Task 2

2 negotiations 3 sign 4 alliance
5 treaty 6 partnership 7 peace
8 member

alpha

Task 1

2 It's in the northwest.
3 It's in the north.
4 It's in the southeast.
5 It's in the east.

Task 2

A Thai
B Swedish, Turkish
C Indian, Latvian
D Sudanese, Japanese
E Israeli
F Algerian, Hungarian, Canadian

bravo

Task 1

2 A few 3 All 4 Most 5 All

charlie

Task 1

2 are you getting 3 are you leaving
4 are you going 5 are you staying

2 a 3 e 4 c 5 b

Task 2

2 at 3 on 4 for 5 in

delta

Task 1

2 By road. 3 By rail. 4 By sea.
5 On foot.

Task 2

4 g 5 d 6 h 7 c 8 j 9 b 10 i

echo

Task 1

2 bathroom 3 TV 4 telephone
5 swimming pool 6 restaurant
7 credit cards

foxtrot

Task 1

2 could 3 Let's 4 don't 5 could

Task 2

2 It's warm with northwest winds. The maximum temperature is 17°C and the minimum is 14°C.
3 It's cloudy with southwest winds. The maximum temperature is 14°C and the minimum is 7°C.
4 It's wet. The maximum temperature is 15°C and the minimum is 4°C.

listening

Task 1

1 plane, 14.30, Nairobi
2 plane, 13.55, Athens
3 train, 11.15, Birmingham and Manchester

Task 2

12.00 press conference
13.30 working lunch
17.30 meeting with General Miles

Task 3

picture b

Task 4

1 b 2 d 3 a 4 c

Unit 9

glossary

Task 3

2 a 3 d 4 e 5 c

alpha

Task 1

2 How often do you eat fast food?
3 How many cigarettes do you smoke a day?
4 How old are you?
5 How much do you weigh?
6 How tall are you?

Task 2

2 He doesn't smoke.
3 He never eats fast food.
4 He does strength exercises about once a week.
5 He's 24 years old.
6 He weighs 79 kilos.

Task 3

2 Smith is heavier than Herter.
3 Smith is more muscular than Herter.
4 Herter is better than Smith at push-ups.
5 Smith is worse than Herter on the assault course.

bravo

Task 1

2 watch TV all day
3 drive everywhere
4 go for a walk
5 relax
6 go for a swim

Possible answers
2 You shouldn't watch TV all day.
3 You shouldn't drive everywhere.
4 You should go for a walk.
5 You should relax.
6 You should go for a swim.

charlie

Task 1

2 meat 3 food 4 dish 5 eat

Task 2

2 less 3 more 4 less 5 more

delta

Task 1

2 c 3 a 4 b 5 c

Task 2

2 Could you bring me some more bread, please?
3 Could you bring me another cup of coffee, please?
4 Could you bring me the bill, please?

Task 3

2 Can I have some more rice, please?
3 Can you pass the water, please?
4 Can I have white coffee, please?

echo

Task 1

1 h   2 b, e   3 d, g   4 a, c

foxtrot

Task 1

2 You mustn't lie the casualty on their side.
3 You must put the casualty's legs at 45°.
4 You must apply a field dressing.
5 You mustn't give the patient any food.

Task 2

2 a   3 b

Task 3

2 d   3 e   4 i   5 l   6 h   7 a   8 k
9 j   10 b   11 c   12 g

listening

Task 1

1 15   2 11   3 21   4 6   5 9   6 7
7 25   8 19

Task 2

First course: Russian salad, green beans, green salad, onion soup
Main course: chicken and chips, steak and chips, Irish stew, spaghetti Bolognese

Task 3

1 a   2 b   3 b

Task 4

Request 1: two casualties, hypothermia, grid 742863, 20 km east of SOLNA
Request 2: one casualty, shooting incident, grid 251905

Task 5

1 heat exhaustion   2 mine victim
3 hypothermia

Unit 10

glossary

Task 2

desert camouflage: oasis, sand dune

woodland / jungle camouflage: forest, grass, jungle, wood

alpha

Task 1

2 e   3 d   4 b   5 f   6 a

Task 2

2 an   3 the   4 the   5 the   6 the
7 the   8 —   9 —   10 A   11 —

Task 3

2 The, the   3 the, the, —
4 The, the, —   5 The, the

bravo

Task 1

2 b   3 c   4 a   5 c

Task 2

2 flattest   3 hilliest   4 widest
5 wettest

charlie

Task 1

2 ravine   3 ridge   4 marsh
5 flat land
2 true   3 false   4 false   5 true

delta

Task 1

2 clean   3 interesting   4 modern
5 quiet

Task 2

2 f   3 d   4 e   5 c   6 a

echo

Task 1

2 on top of   3 over   4 between   5 in

Task 2

2 west   3 northeast   4 northwest
5 southeast   6 south

Task 3

2 d   3 e   4 b   5 a

foxtrot

Task 1

2 move   3 check   4 attack
5 provide   6 remain   7 evacuate

listening

Task 1

1 675798   2 right flank   3 rear

Task 2

1 grid 652908
2 near grid 661907
3 about 250 m to the southeast
4 about 10 km north of here
5 about 10 km south of the objective

Task 3

B2

Task 4

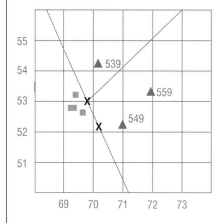

Task 5

2 on top of a hill
3 about 10 km
4 village, river, hill, telegraph wires
5 telegraph wires
6 (usually) southwest

Unit 11

glossary

Task 2

1 ceasefire
2 disarm, demobilise
3 supervise, monitor
4 buffer zone
5 UNMOs, peacekeepers

Task 3

2 Non-Governmental Organisation
3 United Nations Military Observers

alpha

Task 1

2 In 1993.
3 The Secretary General of the United Nations.
4 How countries meet their obligations on human rights.
5 In Geneva, Switzerland.

bravo

Task 1

2 so 3 about 4 like

Task 2

2 a 3 b 4 e 5 c

charlie

Task 1

2 Always 3 Never 4 Always
5 Never

Task 2

2 code 3 opinions 4 host 5 fair
6 neutral 7 patient 8 environment
9 tolerant

delta

Task 1

2 lazy 3 cold 4 reserved

Task 2

1 Excuse me 2 That's OK
3 Congratulations! 4 please

echo

Task 1

2 d 3 a 4 e 5 c

Task 2

2 c 3 d 4 a

foxtrot

Task 1

a visor b prodder d red triangle
e metal detector f trip wires
g mines

2 visor 3 trip wires 4 metal detector
5 prodder 6 red triangle 7 mines

Task 2

Before, First of all, Next, Then, When,
Finally

listening

Task 1

1 km 2 Coy 3 Capt 4 Cpl 5 Col

Task 2

1 NGO 2 VIP 3 UNMO 4 CO
5 UNPROFOR

Task 3

2 0 3 90,000 4 40,000 5 0
6 1,000

Task 4

1 ✔ 2 ✘ 3 ✔ 4 ✘ 5 ✔ 6 ✔

Task 5

1 d 2 a 3 b 4 e 5 c 6 f

Unit 12

glossary

Task 2

rooms: CO's office, Ops room

jobs: chief of staff, staff officer, secretary
general

Task 4

checkpoint, sandbags, tank stops

alpha

Task 1

2 for, to 3 of, to 4 of 5 by

Task 2

2 Head of Mission
3 Force Commander
4 Sector Commander

bravo

Task 1

2 magazine 3 barrel 4 load
5 sights 6 trigger 7 sling 8 bolt

A	R	O	U	N	D	S	L
Q	L	S	J	H	T	L	M
C	O	I	W	Z	R	I	P
M	A	G	A	Z	I	N	E
B	D	H	D	E	G	G	G
O	K	T	N	P	G	V	T
L	F	S	O	K	E	M	B
T	V	B	A	R	R	E	L

Task 2

2 permitted 3 prohibited
4 allowed 5 permitted

charlie

Task 1

2 Hold on
3 Good evening
4 I read back
5 That's correct

Task 2

2 say 3 give 4 be 5 call

delta

Task 1

2 Could you give him a message?
3 Could you tell me the time?
4 Could you show me where the
major's office is?
5 Could you drive us back to HQ?
6 Could you make me a copy of this?

Task 2

1 b 2 c 3 a

echo

Task 1

2 sangar 3 barbed wire 4 car park
5 sentry 6 tank stops

Task 2

2 inside 3 at 4 outside 5 round

foxtrot

Task 1

a CO's office b S1 d briefing room
e bathroom f registry

Task 2

1 d 2 c 3 e 4 a 5 b

listening

Task 1

message 3

Task 2

1 Ops Room duty officer
Lt. Jarvis
Meeting with Major Stanton –
briefing room 0800 hrs tomorrow

2 Sgt. Denton, movement control
Sgt. Clay, Ops room
Sgt Denton will call again later

3 Capt. Robertson, HQ Ops Room
unknown
Alert state will change from red to
yellow at 2359 hrs tonight

Task 3

1 602 358022 2 061 9444
3 527 153572

Task 4

1 all times 2 unload 3 1700
4 Saturday 5 Sunday 6 Combat
7 not allowed 8 Monday 9 Friday
10 0730

Task 5

1 R 2 O 3 R 4 O 5 R

Unit 13

glossary

Task 2

2 start point   3 reporting point
4 release point   5 distance

Task 4

roadblock, rest area, signpost, speed limit, traffic lights

alpha

Task 1

2 d   3 a   4 b   5 e

bravo

Task 1

start point: B   reporting point: E
release point: G

charlie

Task 1

2 Drive, are   3 Check, are
4 Call, can   5 leave, is

Task 2

2 d   3 a   4 b   5 c

delta

Task 1

ACROSS
3 tow   5 boot   7 SW   8 in   9 on
10 report   12 windscreen   13 left
17 limit   20 lights

DOWN
1 exit   2 ton   3 two   4 wet
5 bonnet   6 truck   7 speed   11 rent
12 wheel   14 kit   15 am   16 at
18 in   19 ID

Task 2

2 I'm not going far.
3 I'm sure that will be fine.
4 Just three days, please.
5 Here you are.

echo

Task 1

2 f   3 a   4 e   5 c   6 b

foxtrot

Task 1

2 roger   3 out   4 closing down
5 over   6 read back   7 say again

listening

Task 1

Convoy 2

Task 2

1 July   2 UN   3 1115   4 east
5 third   6 13

Task 3

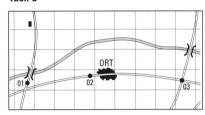

1 0645 hrs   2 0745 hrs   3 0830 hrs
4 0900 hrs

Task 4

1 Radio check   2 OK   3 Out
4 Convoy   5 Roger   6 Closing down
7 Mobile   8 destination

Unit 14

alpha

Task 1

2 set up   3 conduct   4 prevent
5 check

Task 2

2 had   3 mission   4 tasked
5 order

bravo

Task 1

2 e   3 d   4 a   5 b

Task 2

2 in   3 under   4 on   5 at

charlie

Task 1

2 looting   3 cheering   4 shouting

Task 2

2 It looks like a demonstration.
3 They seem to be in the main street.
4 They all seem to be wearing jeans and T-shirts.
5 It's probably about six or seven in the evening.
6 It looks like they're throwing stones.

delta

Task 1

2 What does the man look like?
3 How old is he?
4 How tall is he?
(Possible sentences)
5 She looks hostile.
6 She's slim with long black hair.
7 She's short.
8 She's about 30.

Task 2

2 Which man wants to make a phone call?
3 Which woman does he know?
4 Who lives in the area?
5 Who does she look like?

echo

Task 1

2 Are they wearing blue UN berets?
3 Is that camo face cream waterproof?
4 I have a small brown leather case.
5 This is a wonderful old Swiss knife.
6 It is in the bottom right corner.

foxtrot

Task 1

2 f   3 a   4 c   5 b   6 g   7 d

Task 2

2 a   3 e   4 g   5 f   6 b   7 d

listening

Task 1

5

Task 2

Authorised: 1, 3

Not authorised: 2, 4

Task 3

stove, mess tins, torch, sleeping bags, ammo pouch

Task 4

1 F20   2 sniper   3 857230
4 the corner of   5 two women
6 one man   7 MEDEVAC

Review 2

Task 1

1 c under. It isn't used for radio
   communication.
2 a signpost. It isn't necessary for a
   vehicle to stop here.
3 a trip wires. It isn't a tool used to
   detect and mark the position of
   mines.
4 c track. It isn't a part of a car.
5 d chain of command. It isn't a place.
6 d fog. It isn't a terrain feature.
7 a painkillers. It isn't a health
   complaint.
8 b book. It isn't a part of a rifle.

Task 2

1 blue   2 yellow   3 green and brown
4 red   5 red, white and blue

Task 3

1 b release point
2 b affirmative
3 b enemy
4 a take off
5 a single ticket
6 b unload

Task 4

1 to recce   2 are not permitted   3 to
4 not allowed   5 prohibited to

Task 5

1 in   2 for   3 in   4 at   5 on   6 for
7 to   8 at   9 on   10 round

Task 6

1 safer   2 deepest   3 windier
4 wetter   5 most difficult   6 worst

Task 7

1 before   2 if   3 after   4 unless
5 When

Task 8

2 e   3 a   4 b   5 f   6 d

Task 9

1 shouldn't   2 won't   3 was
4 didn't   5 were

Task 10

1 b   2 d   3 d   4 c   5 d

Tapescript

Unit 1

Task 1 [1]

1 d 2 e 3 j 4 z 5 u

Task 2 [2]

1 an IFV 2 the UN 3 the USA
4 CNN 5 an APC

Task 3 [3]

A: Excuse me, are you Mary Smith?
B: No, I'm not. That's Mary over there.
A: Oh, I'm sorry. What's your name?
B: Barbara. Barbara Stevens.
A: Where are you from, Barbara?
B: Me? I'm from London. Are you American?
A: No, I'm not. I'm from Canada.

Task 4 [4]

0 1 2 3 4 5 6 7 8 9 10 11 12 13 14
15 16 17 18 19 20

Task 5 [5]

There is a column of eleven, twelve, thirteen tanks – yes, thirteen tanks. Then there are three IFVs … three IFVs and … two APCs. Then, there are four jeeps and two trucks, too, and there is also a helicopter. Yes, so thirteen tanks, then three IFVs and two APCs. Then, four jeeps, two trucks and one helicopter.

Task 6 [6]

Good morning. My name is Ivan Danzig. That's Ivan – I -V-A-N Danzig – D-A-N-Z-I-G. I'm a sailor in the Polish navy. I'm nineteen.

Task 7 [7]

Officer: Good morning. Please take a seat.
Liz: Thank you.
Officer: Now I just need some information for the record. So … what's your full name?
Liz: Liz Evans.
Officer: Sorry? Can you spell that?
Liz: Yes, Evans is E-V-A-N-S.
Officer: Oh, Evans! And what's your address?
Liz: The Grand Hotel, London Road.
Officer: And your telephone number?
Liz: My phone number is 616 893542.

Officer: Er … sorry?
Liz: Yes, it's 6-1-6 8-9-3-5-4-2.
Officer: … 3-5-4-2. Are you a journalist?
Liz: Yes, I'm a journalist with the Manchester Post.
Officer: Are you from Manchester?
Liz: Yes, I am.

Unit 2

Task 1 [8]

1 This is NB7. I say again. This is NB7.
2 Calling DR40. I say again. Calling DR40. Do you read me? Over.
3 This is 31AF. We are now at the base. I say again. This is 31AF. We are now at the base. Over.
4 OT125. Meeting at 1500 hours. I say again. OT125. Meeting at 1500 hours. Over.
5 J50. I say again. J50.

Task 2 [9]

1 That's an M60! It's an M60 machine gun! Run!
2 We think they use the AK-47. The Russian Kalashnikov – you know, the AK-47.
3 There are some American rifles in the jeep. Some M16s.
4 A: They train with the G17T.
   B: Pardon?
   A: You know, the Glock – the G17T pistol.

Task 3 [10]

Right lads. This is the afternoon's training schedule: Lunch is from 1200 hours to 1300 hours. There's a first aid class from 1330 hours to 1430 hours, before we go on our foot march at 1440 hours. We finish the foot march at 1640 hours and dinner is at 1700 hours. You have one hour for dinner and then there's a communications class from 1820 hours to 2030 hours. From 2030 hours until 2200 hours you have personal time and then it's Lights Out. Any questions?

Task 4 [11]

Corporal: Do you have any towels, Private O'Brien?

Private: Towels? Yes, I have two towels, Corporal, a toothbrush, some toothpaste and some shampoo.
Corporal: Good. What about soap? Is there any soap in your kit?
Private: Soap, Corporal?
Corporal: Yes, soap, Private O'Brien. Do you have any soap?
Private: Er … no, I don't have any soap, Corporal.
Corporal: Well, you need some soap then. And buy some batteries, too, at the PX.
Private: Batteries, Corporal? But I don't have an electric razor.
Corporal: No, but you have a radio and a torch and batteries are very useful. Right, Private O'Brien. Let's check again. What do you need?
Private: Er … soap and batteries, Corporal.

Task 5 [12]

Well, let's see … er … reveille – that's 'wake up' is at 0600 hours … and then we go to the bathroom immediately – we call this 'personal hygiene' – that's at 0600 hours until 0615 hours – we have fifteen minutes for a wash and shave – and then at 0615 hours we go for breakfast – from 0615 hours until 0640 hours. Then we clean the barrack room – make our beds, clean the toilet areas, put our things away – until 0700 hours. 0700 hours – that's when the sergeant inspects us. It's twenty minutes for barrack inspection and then we start training at 0720 hours. We train from 0720 hours to 1210 hours and then it's time for lunch at 1220 hours. We have one hour for lunch before we start training again.

Unit 3

Task 1 [13]

started, started; trained, trained; served, served; worked, worked; marched, marched; stopped, stopped; finished, finished; celebrated, celebrated; died, died

Task 2 [14]

A: Hi, there. Did you have a good weekend?

B: Yes, I did. It was my son's first birthday.

A: Oh, really? How did you celebrate?

B: We had a big party for him.

A: What did you do last weekend?

B: I went to the club.

A: Oh really? I didn't see you!

Task 3 [15]

Yuri Gagarin was a Russian pilot. He was born near Moscow in Russia in 1934. When he was a boy, he was interested in aircraft and when he was eighteen or nineteen, he joined a local flying club. In 1955, when he was twenty-one, he became a pilot in the Soviet Air Force. His first assignment was at the Soviet Air Force Base in the Arctic.

Gagarin was very intelligent, and soon he was a test pilot for new aircraft. And then he became a cosmonaut at Star City. In 1961, he was the first human in space. The name of his spaceship was Vostock 1. Vostock 1 was in space for about 100 minutes. Yuri was only twenty-seven years old. After this he was a hero.

But Gagarin wasn't happy when he wasn't in a plane and soon he was a test pilot again. He died in an accident in a new MiG-15 in 1968. He was thirty-four years old.

Task 4 [16]

Policeman: OK. Name?

Suspect: Blackmore. Paul Blackmore.

Policeman: Spell your last name.

Suspect: B-L-A-C-K-M-O-R-E.

Policeman: Date of birth?

Suspect: Pardon?

Policeman: How old are you? When were you born?

Suspect: Oh! In 1983.

Policeman: Where?

Suspect: What?

Policeman: Where were you born?

Suspect: Here.

Policeman: In New York?

Suspect: Yes.

Policeman: Are you married?

Suspect: Yes.

Policeman: Do you have any children?

Suspect: Yes, a boy.

Policeman: And how old is he?

Suspect: Three.

Policeman: Right, so … where were you last night at 10 pm?

Suspect: I was at home with my wife.

Policeman: Oh, no, you weren't. You were out in the street.

Suspect: I was not. I was at home with the family. There was a ball game on TV …

Task 5 [17]

Er … well, my name's Jack Truman, and I'm from Sacramento, California. Um … I joined the US Air Force at the age of eighteen, and went straight to Boot Camp for six weeks. Er … that was at Glendale Air Force Base in California. When I graduated six months later, I went to my duty station at Niagara Falls Air Base. Then I was promoted to the rank of airman and deployed to Ramstein Air Base in Germany. That was in 1992. And then I was promoted to the rank of airman 1st class in 1993. Er … in 1995, I requested a transfer to Travis Air Base, in California, because I … um … I, you know, I wanted to be near my family. Um … I really love the Air Force, you know, and I'm very happy with my career.

Unit 4

Task 1 [18]

1 Good morning. I'm here for the conference. My name's Colonel Jennings.

2 Er … good morning. My name's Vickers – Major Vickers.

3 Good morning. This is Lieutenant Shipton. He's here for the conference.

4 Hello. I'm Sergeant Major Williamson …

5 … and this is Captain Stewart. We're here for the conference.

Task 2 [19]

Journalist: Major Pettifer, could you tell us which units are deployed in the area at the moment?

Major: Er … yes, at the moment we have the 1st Armored Brigade, the 2nd Cavalry Regiment, the 18th Airborne Corps, the 5th Infantry Division … er … the 3rd Signal Regiment and, of course, the 14th Artillery Regiment.

Journalist: So, that's the 1st Armored Brigade, the 2nd Cavalry Regiment, the 8th Airborne Corps …

Major: No, the 18th Airborne.

Journalist: Ah, the 18th Airborne Corps, the 5th Infantry Division, the 3rd Signal Regiment and the … er … the 14th Artillery Regiment.

Major: Yes, that's right. The 14th Artillery Regiment.

Task 3 [20]

Let me see. Now, Mrs Hidas from the MOD comes on 2nd December at nine thirty in the morning. Then its Lieutenant Colonel Moore from NATO on 3rd December at seventeen hundred. Finally, we have General Akamoto from the Japanese Defence Force on 5th December at eleven fifteen.

Task 4 [21]

The US Army classifies the different branches of the Army as Combat Arms, Combat Support units and Combat Service Support branches.

The Combat Arms are directly involved in fighting. The Combat arms include Infantry, Armor, Air Defence Artillery, Field Artillery, Aviation, Special Forces and the Corps of Engineers.

Combat Support units provide operational assistance to the Combat Arms and also help with logistics and administration. Combat Support units include the Signal Corps, Military Police Corps, Chemical Corps and Military Intelligence.

The Combat Service Support branches include Transportation, Civil Affairs, Quartermaster, Finance, Army Medical Corps and Ordnance.

Unit 5

Task 1 [22]

There's a man walking down the road. He's wearing a white T-shirt and grey shorts … and trainers. I think he's carrying a bag – yes, he has a bag and he has a cricket bat.

Task 2 [23]

Well, there are three gyms on the ship so I usually work out every day for about thirty minutes, you know, sit ups, and weight-lifting … or sometimes I play basketball or volleyball with the others. Um … let's see … we have a nice swimming pool and I usually go there about once or twice a week, normally in the evenings if I'm free. Um … what else? I often run round the ship – usually in the morning before my watch – and sometimes I play table-tennis with a friend.

Task 3 [24]

First run up the ramp. Then jump over the ditch. After that, crawl under the fence. Then climb up the cargo net. Next jump over the low wall. And finally crawl under the wire and report to me. You have five minutes! Move!

Task 4 [25]

It looks like they're preparing an ambush. Some soldiers are crawling through the long grass to the bridge … I think two of the soldiers are carrying some wire … . Yes, it's wire. They're putting it – wait. I think … yes, it's definitely an ambush …

Unit 6

Task 1 [26]

Lieutenant: OK. Right. Let's start with the flight. Sergeant Thomas, who's responsible for the schedule?
Sergeant: Sergeant Harris, sir.
Lieutenant: And for transport to the airport?
Sergeant: Briggs is in charge of transport, sir, and Corporal Hayne is organising a driver.
Lieutenant: Fine. What about our kit? Who's responsible for checking everything is in order?
Sergeant: The medic is checking the first aid equipment, sir. Sergeant Brooks is responsible for food for the men and Corporal Smith is in charge of maps, GPS and reconnaissance. We are ready to go, sir.
Lieutenant: Thank you, Sergeant Thomas. Good luck!

Task 2 [27]

Journalist 1: What do you think of the situation?
Army press officer: Er … it's difficult at the moment. There's no gas or electricity. The schools and shops are closed. The banks are closed. There's very little food. We need more doctors and medicine. But today the airport is open so there's hope for a solution.
Journalist 2: What do you think of the

people, Colonel? What are they doing?
Army press officer: Oh, the people are fantastic. Everyone is helping …

Task 3 [28]

Right Sergeant Thomas, when we get to the entrance of the town … here … you take Sergeant Briggs and Corporal Hayne and go along the main street – it's called Station Road, but that's not important – until you come to the corner. Take the first right and take up your position opposite the pub. Sergeant Brooks, you, Sergeant Harris and Corporal Smith go round behind the houses … I mean, along here … and cover the entrance to the restaurant here. The rest of you, Corporal Hart and you, the new recruit, what's your name? Right, well, you two come with me. We go along Station Road, behind Sergeant Thomas, Sergeant Briggs and Corporal Hayne, but when they turn right, we go straight on, past the doctor's surgery to the hotel on the second corner. We take up our position here … on this corner, opposite the entrance to the hotel. Does everybody understand? Good.

Task 4 [29]

1 Wow! Just look at your office!
2 Wow! Just look at our office!
3 A: How was the flight?
  B: Not bad!
4 The weather's great!
5 It's a really big city!
6 A: What do you think of those people?
  B: Er, they're OK.

Unit 7

Task 1 [30]

1 To convert inches into centimetres, multiply by 2·54.
2 To convert feet into metres, multiply by 0·3048.
3 To convert miles into kilometres, multiply by 1·609.
4 To convert nautical miles into kilometres, multiply by 1·852.
5 To convert Centigrade into Fahrenheit, multiply by 9, divide by 5 and add 32.

Task 2 [31]

1 Listen, Frankie. Afraid we can't get to you now because it's getting dark. It's too difficult to take a helicopter in. Can you wait until morning?
2 A: This is Sgt Briggs requesting permission to return to base, sir. We couldn't get through. The village was attacked last night and the bridge was blown up.
  B: The bridge? Damn! Permission granted …
3 A: Hello D99. This is A30. Message. Over.
  B: D99. Send. Over.
  A: A30. Message. We can't establish contact with base. The telephone lines are all down. We think they were cut by the enemy. Over.
4 Hello? Jack? Listen. Can you send a vehicle? The jeep's in the ditch! About ten kilometres outside the village, just near the bridge. OK. Fine. Thanks a lot. Bye.

Task 3 [32]

We now move on to the Black Hawk. This helicopter has a crew of three and can carry up to eleven fully equipped troops – so, that's a crew of three and eleven troops. It weighs 11,780 pounds and has a maximum height of 16 feet 9 inches – that's 16 feet 9 inches from the ground to the top of the rotor blade. It can cruise at 5,000 feet with a maximum speed of 162 knots … er, 162 knots and has a range of 304 – three-zero-four – 304 nautical miles. It can fly very close to the ground or at a maximum height of 19,000 feet.

Task 4 [33]

The Black Hawk is manufactured by the Sikorsky Aircraft Corporation, based in Connecticut in the States. It is also produced in Japan and Korea. It is designed to carry troops into battle and to serve as a logistical support aircraft, but all missions are possible – troop assault, combat support, combat service support. It can also be used for special operations, for example, medical evacuation, search and rescue, and command and control.

The helicopter can carry a weight of 9,000 pounds outside and can be armed with a variety of missiles, including the

Hellfire anti-armour missile, and also rockets, machine guns and 20 mm cannons. In addition, 7.62 mm or 50 calibre machine guns can be mounted in the windows.

The Black Hawk can fly very close to the ground and can tolerate small arms fire. And it can't be detected very easily. That is why it is used to transport troops into the combat zone. It can also fly in almost any weather condition. Finally, it is equipped with voice, satellite, UHF and VHF communication systems, and also IFF (which means *identification friend or foe*).

Unit 8

Task 1 [34]

1 Flight IB 7905 to Nairobi at 14.30 now boarding at Gate 5. Flight IB 7905 to Nairobi at 14.30 now boarding at Gate 5.

2 Last call for a Mr Dax. Please go to Gate 7 for your flight at 13.55 to Athens. I repeat: last call for Mr Dax on BA flight 4813 to Athens at 13.55. Please go immediately to Gate 7 as your plane is ready to leave.

3 The train now arriving at platform 9 is the 11.15 to Birmingham and Manchester. The train now arriving at platform 9 is the 11.15 to Birmingham and Manchester.

Task 2 [35]

Sir, you have a very busy agenda next week. On Monday morning, at ten o'clock, you are meeting the Secretary General from the National Union for talks, before the press conference at twelve o'clock. You're having a working lunch with members of the local council at 1.30 and then, in the afternoon, there is a meeting with the Chief of Police at four pm. At 5.30 General Miles is coming to see you in your office and then at six thirty …

Task 3 [36]

Well, it looks like another cold day tomorrow! In the morning, we are expecting fog, particularly in the valleys, and low temperatures – down to 2° C in the north and northeast – but not so cold as we go further east – with some snow on the mountains. In the south, and also in western parts of the country, we can expect some rain and temperatures of around 6 °. So that's low temperatures and fog or snow in the north and northeast, becoming slightly warmer as we move east, and higher temperatures in the south and west of the country, with showers around lunchtime.

Task 4 [37]

1 The convoy is leaving KUDINE tomorrow morning at 0600 hours. Estimated time of arrival at HQ is 0830 hours. I repeat. Estimated time of arrival at HQ is 0830 hours.

2 Listen, this is Charlie speaking. Desert Rat is meeting WZ at the Black Lion tomorrow at 8.30 pm. Have you got that?

3 This is B5D requesting permission to land. There's a storm coming. I say again. B5D requesting permission to land. A storm is coming.

4 Hello? … Listen, we're staying at the Hotel President. Room 38. Why don't you come over for a drink?

Unit 9

Task 1 [38]

A: Right, let's see. There are fifteen cans of peaches, eleven cans of pears, twenty-one cans of tomatoes and…

B: Sorry? How many cans of tomatoes did you say?

A: Twenty-one, and six – only six cans of beans. Then we have … er nine – nine jars of coffee.

A: Nine jars of coffee. OK. What about honey? How many jars of honey are there?

B: Er … honey. Five, six … there are seven jars of honey. And now lentils … twenty-five jars of lentils …

A: Twenty-five?

B: Yes, that's right. Twenty-five jars of lentils and nineteen jars of black beans …

Task 2 [39]

For the first course on the menu today, we have Russian salad, green beans, green salad, and onion soup. And for the main course, there's chicken and chips, steak and chips, Irish stew and spaghetti Bolognese.

Task 3 [40]

Interviewer: So, Doctor, could you tell us what we should do in this situation?
Doctor: Well, the first thing you should do is to put the patient on their side. Never lie them on their back – always on their side and do not cover them with anything. Don't put a blanket over them, or a coat or anything like that because they must keep cool. It's very important to keep their temperature down. So don't cover them up with anything at all. And you shouldn't give them any food, either – just drinks like water or warm tea or something like that.
Interviewer: So basically there are three important things to remember in this situation then: firstly, to put the person on their side, not on their back. Second, you shouldn't cover them with anything, and last of all, only to give them something to drink, but nothing to eat.
Doctor: Yes, that's it, exactly.

Task 4 [41]

REQUEST 1
A: Hello, A14. This is R24. CASEVAC. Over.

B: A14. Send. Over.

A: R24.
ALPHA – R24
BRAVO – grid 742863. Twenty kilometres east of SOLNA, I Spell: SIERRA, OSCAR, LIMA, NOVEMBER, ALPHA.
CHARLIE – grid 742863
DELTA – 24 Field Hospital.
ECHO – Two casualties with hypothermia requiring urgent medical attention.
FOXTROT – Area is secure. Approach from the west. Over.

B: A14. Roger. Question. Do you have a Doctor? Over.

A: R24. Negative. We need a doctor and an ambulance. Over.

REQUEST 2 [42]
A: Hello DL7. This is R50. CONTACT. Wait. Out. … Hello DL7. This is R50. CONTACT at 1920 hours at grid 251905. Shooting incident. One casualty with chest wound. Request urgent MEDEVAC. Over.

B: DL7. Is the area secure? Over.

A: R50. Area is secure. There are no hostile elements in the area. Over.

B: DL7. Roger. We are sending an air medical evacuation team now. Over.

A: R50. Roger. Out.

Task 5 [43]

1

A: Sir! We have a man down, sir!

B: What's wrong, Jackson?

A: It's Smith, sir. He's on the ground. He can't get up, sir. He can't move and he can't say anything, sir.

B: It's the sun! It's very strong today. Move him out of the sun. Take him over there where it's cooler. Take his pack and his belt off and lie him on his back. Put a wet towel over him and watch him.

A: Yes, sir!

2

A: What have we got here? Bring the patient in here!

B: A leg wound, doctor. The patient stepped on a mine – lucky to be alive! But it was very bad. His friend put a rope round the leg and called us.

A: Did you put this bandage on?

B: Yes, we did. And we gave him a painkiller and took his temperature – it's very high.

A: OK, thank you. The patient must go straight to the operating theatre …

3

A: This is Dr Patel speaking. Listen. We're sending a helicopter right now but this is what you should do until it gets to you. OK?

B: Yes, I understand doctor.

A: Right. Is your friend conscious? Is he awake?

B: Yes. Yes, he is, but he looks very white.

A: Yes, well, don't worry. You should keep him warm – put your jacket round him or a blanket or something and give him a hot drink. OK? But don't give him any food – nothing to eat. Is that clear?

B: Yes, doctor, I understand. I should give him a hot drink, but nothing to eat.

A: Yes, that's right. Perfect. And lie him on his back and make sure he is warm. Don't worry. The helicopter's on its way right now.

Unit 10

Task 1 [44]

Right, men, these are your orders for the assault. 1st platoon will deploy in firing positions at grid 675798. I say again. 1st platoon will deploy in firing positions at grid 675798. 2nd platoon will assault the position from the right flank and 3rd platoon will remain in reserve 100 metres to the rear of the LZ. OK. Is that understood? 1st platoon will deploy in firing positions at grid 675798, 2nd platoon will assault the position from the right flank and 3rd platoon will remain in reserve 100 metres to the rear of the LZ. OK, men. Let's move out!

Task 2 [45]

1 The Communications Centre is located at grid 652908. That's the Communications Centre at grid 652908.

2 There is an enemy tank in the vicinity of grid 661907. I say again. An enemy tank is moving near grid 661907.

3 We think there is a minefield about 250 m to the southeast. That's a minefield about 250 m to the south east of our position.

4 There are some friendly forces about 10 km north of here. I say again. Friendly forces are located about 10 km north of here.

5 Our current location is about 10 km south of the objective. I say again. Our current location is about 10 km south of the objective.

Task 3 [46]

I am now flying over the area, going north and I have the wood on my right – that's a wood to the east. I can see the river straight ahead going east–west. I say again. There's a river straight ahead going east–west. There are two low buildings on the other side of the river, about 100 m apart …Yes, I am approaching two low buildings about 100 m apart on the other side of the river …

Task 4 [47]

OK. So this is the latest report we have from the recce platoon. There are some enemy forces in the region. A platoon-size unit is located at hill 549, in the vicinity of grid 710521. They have a protective minefield about 250 m southwest of the hill and another minefield about 500 m to the northwest. So, two minefields in the area: one about 250 m to the southwest of the hill, and a second one about half a kilometre to the northwest. Other enemy units are located …

Task 5 [48]

A: Captain García will now brief you on the landing zone. Captain García?

B: Thank you, Commander. Well, the LZ is grass. It is an area of grass, located on top of a hill, about 10 km north of SKALE, the nearest village. From here, you will fly over the village of SKALE first and then about 10 km further north you will see the landing zone on the hill, right in front of you. There is a river in the valley at the bottom of the hill and there are telegraph wires going up the hill from the village. Watch out for these wires! Finally, winds. The winds are usually southwest. So you will normally have the wind behind you when you reach the LZ. I think that's about all I can tell you. Any questions?

Unit 11

Task 1 [49]

1 kilometre
2 company
3 captain
4 corporal
5 colonel

Task 2 [50]

1 NGO
2 VIP
3 UNMO
4 CO
5 UNPROFOR

Task 3 [51]

Journalist: Sir, could you tell us what the situation is like in the capital city at the moment?

UN representative: Er … well, I think this is one of the quickest and fastest UN missions I know of! To start with education: we now have 400 schools open and ready to receive 100,000 children next week. This is not an easy situation but classes will start next week in most places. As I said, there are now 400 schools open.

Journalist: And what about the public utilities? Is there any electricity or running water?

UN representative: Yes, in the capital city we have most services operating now, including telecommunications and the post office – and tomorrow the rubbish will be collected for the first time in five months! But in the villages – only 10 km away there is no phone, no TV and no radio. Life is still extremely difficult for the villagers.

Journalist: Uh-huh. But are many people returning now?

UN representative: Yes, I think so … Yes, definitely. There are about 90,000 refugees coming back by plane from various countries …

Journalist: I'm sorry, sir, did you say 19,000 or 90,000?

UN representative: 90,000 – that's 90,000 refugees returning by plane and about 300,000 more are returning over land from the north. We must not forget that more than 40,000 homes were destroyed. 40,000 houses must be built again! That means 40,000 families have nowhere to live at the moment and there are no jobs, no banks are open. But UNHCR (the United Nations High Commissioner for Refugees), UNICEF and the World Health Organisation are working together to re-build houses and provide help, and by next winter, I hope we will have the situation under control.

Journalist: And finally, what about security? Is there still a lot of crime in the city?

UN representative: Well, the situation is getting much better. The mission is now responsible for police duties and we now have 1,000 UN police officers – a thousand international police officers from the UN – and 450 of these thousand officers are deployed in the capital city and so now there is more safety on the streets. We also have protection forces in the villages.

Journalist: Thank you very much, sir. We wish you every success with the mission.

Task 4 [52]

My typical day was to get up at 6 am and to check with the soldiers that there was no fighting between the two sides in the buffer zone during the night. This was important because there were villages between the two sides – on both sides of the border we were patrolling – and these people were often attacked. Before I could go into the villages assigned to my platoon along the border, the roads and tracks needed to be swept for mines every day for six months. This was very tiring – it was very hot out in the midday sun – and also very stressful – several of my men died as a result of this daily routine looking for mines everywhere and others were severely injured. Er … then, when the roads were clear, the villagers – the refugees – could return to their homes and go about their daily tasks, and generally get on with their lives. We visited them with the platoon medic and if there was a serious illness or problem, we would call a doctor from the main camp to come to the village by helicopter or armoured vehicle.

Task 5 [53]

CO: … and it's now over to Major Thompson, who will explain the rules of engagement for the mission. Major Thompson?

Major: Thank you, sir. Right, well, as you all know, the first rule to remember is that all military operations should be conducted according to the laws of war. I think everyone knows this and it is not really necessary to repeat but it is very important. So, rule number one: conduct all military operations according to the laws of war.

Secondly, all necessary action should be taken by the CO for the unit to be ready for self-defence at all times. This means that rifles should be kept clean, all vehicles should be maintained for immediate use, and so on, so that the unit can defend itself at all times.

Thirdly, peacekeeping forces will only open fire if they are fired upon. I repeat: peacekeeping forces will only open fire if they are fired upon. They will never open fire against anyone unless they are attacked first. Is that clear? Right. So, only open fire if you are under attack.

Rule number four: Only the minimum force required to carry out the mission will be used. Remember, it is very easy to forget what is happening or where you are under stress, but a soldier – and particularly a soldier from the UN peacekeeping forces can never use more than the minimum force required to carry out the mission. Is that understood?

The last two rules of engagement refer to treatment of the local people. Rule number 5: All people should be treated with respect. This rule is for everyone: other peacekeepers, local police, civilians and also hostile persons. Remember, you are here as a peacekeeper and you must show respect to everyone … and finally, rule number six: Civilians can only be detained for security reasons or in self-defence. This refers specifically to these hostile elements. You can only detain such persons if they are firing at you, and your life – or the life of others – is at risk, that is to say, only in self-defence or to protect the civilian population.

Unit 12

Task 1 [54]

A: We're having a dinner in the Sergeants' Mess on Tuesday. Would you like to come?

B: Yes, sure. What do I have to wear?

A: It's dress uniform.

B: OK, fine. What time should I be there?

A: Can you get there for eight?

Task 2

1 [55]

This is a message for Lt Jarvis from the Ops Room duty officer. There's a meeting with Major Stanton in the briefing room at 0800 hours tomorrow morning.

2 [56]

A: Good morning, Ops Room.

B: Good morning. This is Sergeant Denton from movement control. I'd like to speak to Sergeant Clay.

A: I'm sorry, Sergeant Clay isn't in the office at the moment. He'll be back at approximately 1030 hours.

B: At 1030 hours? OK. Can you tell him I'll call back?

A: Yes, I'll let Sergeant Clay know that Sergeant Denton will him call later.

B: That's correct. Thank you.

A: Thank you, goodbye.

3 [57]

A: This is Captain Robertson at HQ Ops Room. I'm calling to inform you that the Alert State will change from red to yellow at 2359 hours tonight.

B: I read back. The Alert State will change from red to yellow at 2359 hours tonight.

A: That's correct.

Task 3 [58]

1 For ring tones you can really identify with! We have *your* type of sound! Just dial 602 358022 and download direct from our list. That's 602 358022, for a personal ring tone!

2 Can you help? If you were in or near the town of Goric last Tuesday evening between 6 and 8 pm, please phone this number: 061 9444. Your information could be vital! That's 061 9444.

3 We couldn't contact the family. Could you try again later? The number to ring is 527 153572. I'll repeat that for you: 527 153572. Thank you.

Task 4 [59]

Right men. These are the Camp Orders so pay attention. First of all, weapons. Weapons should be carried at all times in the 'unload' position. I repeat: always carry your weapon in the 'unload' position. Is that understood? Second: Commanders Brief. Commander's brief is at 1700 hours Monday to Saturday and at 1800 hours on Sunday. That's 1700 hours from Monday to Saturday and at 1800 hours on Sunday. Next, Dress. Combat uniform should be worn at all times on the camp. So I don't want to see any tracksuits. OK? Only combat uniform at all times. That brings us on to the subject of alcohol. For security reasons, alcohol is not allowed on the camp. Is that clear to everyone? Absolutely no alcohol is allowed on the camp. And finally, work parties. There will be work parties on Monday, Wednesday and Friday from 0730 hours to 1200 hours. I'll repeat that: work parties will be organised on Monday, Wednesday and Friday from 0730 hours to 1200 hours. Any questions?

Task 5 [60]

1 Could you bring me the report?
2 Take this message over to Captain Blackmore.
3 Can you sign here?
4 Sit down, please.
5 Corporal, could you bring me the map?

Unit 13

Task 1 [61]

Good afternoon. I'm Lieutenant Zumikis and I'm here to brief you on tomorrow's convoy operation. Our mission is to escort a humanitarian aid convoy from the airport to the village of IX. The convoy is composed of five 5-ton trucks with food, drinking water, blankets and medical supplies. We will provide an armed escort with four APCs. I'll be in an APC at the front of the convoy, and I'll be followed by the first two trucks. Another APC will follow behind the first two trucks, and the other two APCs will be at the rear of the convoy, behind the other three trucks. I'll just repeat the order again: my APC, followed by two trucks, and then the second APC. Then the other three trucks and finally two more APCs at the rear of the convoy. Is that clear to everybody?

Task 2 [62]

Good morning. My name's Captain Hidas and I'm here to brief you on the convoy operation on 2nd July – the day after tomorrow. Our mission is to escort a UN convoy from KALE to the village of DORF. We will leave KALE at 0700 hours and our estimated time of arrival at DORF is 1115 hours. Our start point is the A5 out of KALE going east. We will continue along the A5 for about five kilometres until we reach the roundabout. At the roundabout, we need to take the third exit for the B35. The exit is signposted so there is no problem. We will continue along the B35 until we reach the junction with the B33, where we will turn left. Our reporting point is at a bridge about thirteen kilometres down the road. We will then cross the bridge and have a ten-minute rest at the service station on the other side. When we leave the rest area, …

Task 3 [63]

Right, everyone. This is the mission for tomorrow so listen. We will leave the airport at 0600 hours and the whole movement will take about three hours. The total distance of our route is about 100 kilometres. We'll join the humanitarian aid trucks at DUNE airport at grid 439102. This is the start point. All vehicles in the convoy will come under my command when we reach the start point.

We'll take the A6, signposted ORT, south from DUNE airport and stop to report three times during the movement. We'll stop for a ten-minute rest when we reach the first reporting point, O1, just after the bridge over the River Pil. Our ETA at O1 is 0645 hours.

When you leave O1, turn left onto the B12, signposted ORT. Our second reporting point, O2, is a petrol station on the B12 just before the village of ORT. Our Estimated Time of Arrival at O2 is 0745 hours. The third, and final reporting point, O3, will be at the junction of the B12 with the B14, about thirty-five kilometres after the village of ORT. Our Estimated Time of Arrival at O3 is 0830 hours. That's 0830 hours at O3.

Then when you leave O3, continue along the B12 until you reach the roundabout at the junction with the B19. Take the exit signposted IX. Our estimated time of arrival at IX is 0900 hours.

Task 4

1 [64]

A: Hello D1, this is R3. Radio check. Over.

B: D1. OK. Over.

A: R3. OK. Out.

2 [65]

A: Hello D1, this is R3. Leaving Z1 in Convoy. Now mobile from Z1. Over.

B: D1. Roger. Out.

3 [66]

A: Hello D1, this is R3. Closing down for thirty minutes at Z2. Over.

B: D1. Roger. Out.

4 [67]

R3: Hello D1, this is R3. Mobile from Z2 destination Z3. Over.

D1: D1. Roger. Out.

Unit 14

Task 1 [68]

There's a man on the right in the front of the crowd – he looks very suspicious. I think he's carrying a gun under his jacket. He has a beard and short grey hair, medium-height, and middle-aged. He's probably about forty-five or fifty years old – certainly over forty, I think. He seems very impatient. It looks like he's waiting for a sign or an order …

Task 2 [69]

Your mission is to patrol the area in the immediate vicinity of the bridge during daylight hours and to keep the area clear of snipers. Your rules of engagement are as follows.

First, do not use deadly force or open fire unless your life or the life of others is in immediate danger. Remember you are UN peacekeepers, not an attacking force, so no force is authorised unless it is to protect yourself or other people.

Now, with respect to the bridge: You are not authorised to use deadly force to stop or disarm persons crossing the bridge unless they are engaged in hostile acts. This is really the same as ROE number 1: no deadly force unless lives are in danger. Hostile acts include threatening to use a weapon. This means, if a person threatens to shoot you with a rifle or attack you with a knife, etc. then you can use your weapon to protect yourself. Is that understood?

OK. But remember: Always give a challenge in English first and then in the local language before you open fire.

Now, what about vehicles? Well, civilian vehicles may not normally be attacked – unless they attempt to drive straight over the bridge and then you are only authorised to fire warning shots and then to shoot at the tyres if these vehicles do not stop at the checkpoint, unless of course you are fired on. So do not shoot at civilian vehicles to kill. Only fire warning shots if they do not stop at a checkpoint and always give a challenge first – in English and in the local language. Then, if they don't stop, fire at the tyres of the vehicle.

So, I repeat: deadly force is only authorised if your life or the lives of others are in immediate danger.

Task 3 [70]

A: Hello L2. This is F21. Message. Over.

B: F21. Send. Over.

A: L2. Reporting recent movement of hostile elements in wood at grid 253755. We have a stove, two mess tins, a torch, two sleeping bags and a small, brown, empty ammo pouch. I say again: there is a stove, two mess tins, a torch, two sleeping bags and a small, brown, empty ammo pouch. It looks like two members of the militia were here a few hours ago. It seems they left the vicinity very fast. We are conducting a reconnaissance of the area. Over.

B: F21. Is the situation under control? Over.

A: L2. Affirmative. Over.

B: F21. Report in ten minutes. Over.

A: L2. Wilco. Over.

B: F21. Roger. Out.

Task 4 [71]

A: Hello E2. This is F20. CONTACT. Wait. Out. (pause) … Hello E2. This is F20. CONTACT at grid 857230. Sniper fire from the corner of Main Street and Sea Road onto civilian population. Returned fire and killed sniper. There are civilian casualties, two women badly injured and one civilian man dead. Request MEDEVAC. Over.

B: E2. Is the situation under control? Over.

A: F20. Affirmative. There are no hostile elements in the area. Over.

B: E2. Roger. We are sending an ambulance immediately. Confirm you will be staying at the location. Over.

A: F20. Affirmative. Over.

B: E2. Roger. Out.